T0273996

Praise for

CustomHer Experience

"*CustomHer Experience* helps teach brands how to attract and retain the most influential buyer. Mares shares how to create experience epiphanies, which fill a gap for the customer that they didn't know and now cannot live without."

—John R. DiJulius III, author of *The Relationship Economy*

"*CustomHer Experience* is important to being successful in *any* business. Katie Mares provides practical ways to 'think like the female consumer' that will help you unlock the female buying power. It is imperative for businesses to think through and design customer experiences and processes using *her* lens. In these pages, you'll find scientifically-back information combined with easily actionable tactics that all businesses from any industry can put to use. This is a must-read if you want to capture the heart and mind of who may potentially be your most influential customer: the woman."

—Shep Hyken, customer service/experience expert and *NYT* and
WSJ best-selling author of *The Amazement Revolution*

"Mares provides a stunningly thorough analysis of how to reach and retain women shoppers at every touchpoint. This is an essential read for anyone looking to transform their business by building a customer experience tailored to a woman's needs and expectations in a way that's more than skin deep."

—Peter Giorgi, CMO of Celebrity Cruises

CUSTOM*Her*
EXPERIENCE

CUSTOM*Her*
EXPERIENCE

○⚲

THE IMPORTANCE OF TAILORING

YOUR BRAND EXPERIENCE

TO THE FEMALE CONSUMER

GREENLEAF
BOOK GROUP PRESS

This publication is designed to provide accurate and authoritative information in regard to the subject matter covered. It is sold with the understanding that the publisher and author are not engaged in rendering legal, accounting, or other professional services. Nothing herein shall create an attorney-client relationship, and nothing herein shall constitute legal advice or a solicitation to offer legal advice. If legal advice or other expert assistance is required, the services of a competent professional should be sought.

Published by Greenleaf Book Group Press
Austin, Texas
www.gbgpress.com

Distributed by Greenleaf Book Group

For ordering information or special discounts for bulk purchases, please contact Greenleaf Book Group at PO Box 91869, Austin, TX 78709, 512.891.6100.

Design and composition by Greenleaf Book Group and Brian Phillips
Cover design by Greenleaf Book Group and Brian Phillips

Publisher's Cataloging-in-Publication data is available.

Print ISBN: 979-8-88645-026-2

eBook ISBN: 979-8-88645-027-9

Part of the Tree Neutral® program, which offsets the number of trees consumed in the production and printing of this book by taking proactive steps, such as planting trees in direct proportion to the number of trees used: www.treeneutral.com

TreeNeutral

Printed in the United States of America on acid-free paper

22 23 24 25 26 27   10 9 8 7 6 5 4 3 2 1

First Edition

To my girls, Ela, little Riley, Maddie, Regan, and big Riley.
I hope you know you can have your cake and eat it too.

To my boys, Noah, Jaden, and Rhett.
My wish is to watch you grow and support the
women around you, so they can have their cake and eat it too.

To the man who lifts me up,
inspires me daily, helps me bake my cake, then eats it with me!
Thayne, I didn't know what love was until I met you.

To the daring ones. Be bold, be different, be YOU.

CONTENTS

PREFACE

$\mathcal{N}$ot long ago, I decided I needed a second car. Notice the word *I* in that sentence. *I*—a woman, mom, daughter, and businesswoman—made the decision to make this large purchase. But more on that later.

Each night, for the better part of a month, after the kids were in bed, I would carefully comb the web for our next family vehicle. I looked online at all the different makes, models, prices, and brands. I needed the space for me, my three kids, their friends, and my son's very smelly hockey equipment, which explains why I was drawn immediately to the big SUVs that sat at least seven and had a third row of seats that could fold down for more cargo space. Excited about the multitude of options I had, I soon realized that *every* brand seemed to have a model that fit my criteria list. It was fun spending countless hours on websites building my dream SUV, adding and taking away features to fit my budget. However, I had an ominous feeling that my sense of enjoyment would be coming to an end as soon as I entered the dealership—in person. As a *woman*.

I've been a brand experience expert for close to fifteen years, and I know what I'm doing, but as a female, I still anticipated a less-than-stellar encounter. The last time I'd purchased a vehicle, I'd been shocked at the way people at the dealership had treated me—as if I knew nothing and held no buying power—and I wasn't going to be taken by surprise this time. Preparation was key, so I researched and strategized my approach. Or at least that's what I thought.

When I pulled up to the dealership, armed with all of my research, I turned to my three kids in the backseat to give them the "please behave" talk, to which they dutifully nodded before making a mad dash for the showroom, bursting through its doors as I hurried after them (my talk clearly had zero impact on them—go figure!). My kids were more excited than I was for this moment. For them, it meant being able to play in shiny new cars. I was already cringing at the sounds of car doors slamming, worrying about crushed fingers and the disapproving glances of salespeople.

In spite of all this, I was excited to have the opportunity to put my research into action, breathe in the new car smell, and possibly purchase a vehicle. Inside, I stood a few moments in the middle of the showroom, waiting for someone to help me, before glancing over at my kids, who were circling a sporty black-on-black number, playing cops and robbers (or some sort of loud game) around its bumper. A middle-aged man was also inspecting the sports car while dodging my children, and I noticed a smiling salesman already approaching him, hand outstretched in greeting.

I stood by myself for five more minutes, but when no salesperson came my way, I began following my kids from car to car.

Finally, after about seventeen minutes—but who was counting?—a young man from the dealership approached, his eyes moving from me to my kids, who were all packed into a car, honking the horn, laughing and yelling at each other. The salesman's eyes widened, and he gave a big exhale as he came closer. I could hear the thoughts swimming around in his head: *Great, another mom and her kids.* He continued to saunter over (it felt like I was witnessing a slow-motion sequence in a movie) and stopped about three feet in front of me. He looked quite concerned.

"Um, ma'am? Are you doing okay?" he asked, before looking around the rest of the showroom. "Is your husband here?"

I narrowed my eyes. "Well, I'm the one who—"

"Should we call him over?" he asked me without making eye contact.

I raised my eyebrows and frowned at him, but the young man ignored my folded arms and tapping foot, still searching for the man of the house—the assumed purchaser. He ignored my puzzled expression and negative body language. I felt sick to my stomach, even a bit light-headed, as the sad realization hit me: We're in the twenty-first century, and women are still being overlooked as influential, competent consumers with strong buying power—who are also keenly discerning.

The salesman still hadn't asked me my name or attempted to uncover what I was looking for in a vehicle—all because I was a woman.

I finally locked my eyes with his and said, "*I* will be purchasing this vehicle. *I* am the one you should be serving." His eyes grew wider and a slow smile stretched across his face, but before he could speak, I continued. "But I won't be buying it from you."

Rounding up my kids, I headed for the door, leaving the salesman in the dust. In a swift few seconds we'd left the dealership—kids and all. We piled into our car and I turned to my kids.

"Can you believe that?"

My daughter shrugged her shoulders. "Believe what?"

Now *my* eyes were wide. "How that sales associate behaved? He completely ignored me and wouldn't even speak to me because I was a woman."

I suppose my kids must have seen the steam blowing out of my ears or my face turning red, because they all looked suitably horrified.

"Let's get out of here," I said, backing out of the parking lot.

At each of the three dealerships we visited later that afternoon, my experience was identical. Each salesman nonchalantly wandered over to me, eventually, but only to ask where my husband was, never thinking to engage me as the purchaser.

I went home that day feeling deflated, disappointed, and honestly, confused. What had happened? I'd been informed and prepared, feeling excited. All I'd wanted to do was to give a lot of my money to a dealership that I respected. Was that such a tall order to fill? Apparently so, in my case.

Later that evening, I thought even more about what had happened. As a brand experience expert, I was shocked at the disconnect between the "service" (if you could even call it that) and the ticket price of the item up for purchase. I knew that from a sales standpoint, next to a home, a car was the second-largest purchase the average person tends to make. But as a woman, I was appalled at how poorly I'd been treated. In an age when women own over nine million businesses, employ more than eight million people, and generate $1.4 trillion in sales—all while raising kids and keeping up a household—we are still mostly disregarded when it comes to being respected as purchasers, for both small and big-ticket items.[1]

So I began my investigation. I hopped on Amazon and ordered every book I could find on the customer experience and the female consumer. Not to my surprise, there weren't very many. I then scoured the Internet for every article and website I could find that pertained to women as influencers.

I started to see, not only from statistical, but also experiential, points of view, that an organization's brand experience can often be disjointed and inconsistent, especially when it comes to the female customer. After months of reading and hours of conversations with female employees and customers, I was ready to draw my own conclusions on what was causing this enormous experience gap that women undergo when purchasing from businesses. More important, I saw patterns emerge, which showed me how to transform the very black and white, non-emotionally driven service a woman currently receives into the alluring, interactional and emotionally focused experience she craves.

Even if a business is sound in an operational sense (they get all the steps right), it might struggle with how to create a successful experience in an interactional sense. Most businesses have a process to deliver the service they provide. Unfortunately, very few businesses focus on elevating "interaction" so that a brand experience includes a personal connection with the consumer, addressing their genuine interests and needs.

As a woman and an authority in this area, I recognize that the branding disconnect is a problem not only for female consumers, who often feel misunderstood, but also for businesses that lose potential sales *and* women's loyalty.

It's fascinating (and disheartening) to me that while the female movement has definitely infiltrated our social world—and while we preach "girl power" everywhere—this mindset hasn't penetrated business branding, or the experience businesses provide to women. Ignoring the world's most influential consumer is an approach that undermines a brand and breeds distrust in female customers, today and in the future.

I'm a woman and an entrepreneur, so the concern of equality has always tugged at my core. I strongly believe that women can have their cake and eat it too. Businesses also need to accept, fundamentally, the fact that women are incredibly valuable assets—not only as employees but also as consumers. Businesses *must* align with this vision if they want to thrive and grow with the times. Of course, I am also a realist and know this change won't happen overnight.

I offer to you the words in this book, based on my research and experiences as a woman, so you can become stronger and more aligned with how to treat your female consumers, who are essentially the core of your business.

After my horrific car-buying experience, I set out to prove that the definitive decision maker in most households is the woman, and she should be treated as such. I knew I had to share my findings (the inside scoop on *her*) with business leaders, to show why and how they must reach this undervalued female consumer market.

Do you want to know how my car search ended? I visited seven dealerships and spent over two months searching for the right second vehicle. I ended up buying from Hyundai, an unexpected brand that offered me a great experience. From the moment I walked into the Hyundai dealership, I felt valued as a customer, regardless of my gender. The team greeted me with a smile, called me by name, made sure my kids had fun, and most important, uncovered my needs before working tirelessly to deliver on them. I spent less than I had budgeted, made some great relationships, and got a car with all the bells and whistles. It should be noted that I bought from there not because of the price, quality, or brand name. I bought from there because of the buying experience. As a female, I valued that above all else. I couldn't help it—as a woman, I'm hardwired that way!

Purchasing a second car was the best and worst experience I'd ever had, all at the same time. The process was strenuous, deflating, and just plain frustrating. The end result, however, was an awakening to an unfulfilled need—a delivery gap in businesses that I could help close. Ultimately, my car-shopping experience brought me here to you. It opened my eyes and gave me the drive I needed to inspire positive, actionable change in those who provide the experiences female consumers encounter. For that, I am grateful.

Of course, I don't hold a magic wand, but you do. I will give you the insights, tools, and guidance you need to ignite the spark within you and your team. The true power comes when you accept the need for change and focus on providing a brand and consumer experience women can't live without. When you start doing that—and doing it well—you will cultivate trust, build loyalty, earn referrals, and make top-line sales. Your female customers will experience something completely unique in the relationship you offer, and they won't want to go anywhere else.

Now let's create that experience together and make change happen!

THE FUTURE OF RETAIL

---

*I*n ancient times, strong women like Cleopatra, Boudicca, and Esther were recorded in the history books as revered rulers and warriors, standing shoulder to shoulder with their male counterparts. But in the fourth and fifth centuries AD, women began taking a backseat as the world defined and encouraged a female's role solely as homemaker. Women couldn't vote, were discouraged from owning businesses or property, and were not given the opportunity to make strides in an increasingly male-dominated world.

One thing, though, has never changed: Women do, and will continue to, influence all household purchases. Women are the Chief Purchasing Officers in their households and the most influential consumers in the world. We are the economy of the United States. As women have become more educated, with far more financial strength and decision-making abilities, their earning power has grown exponentially.

According to *Inc.*, "Women earn more higher-education degrees than men and start new businesses at a faster rate. Women's earning power is growing faster than men's. And women now make up more than half of Twitter users and Facebook subscribers."[1]

In fact, according to the Inclusionary Leadership Group, women make or influence 83 percent of all non-business-to-business consumer purchases.[2] Not only do females hold veto power on the majority of purchasing decisions, they are a business's number one referral source! According to Gender Marketing Strategies, women are 25 to 30 percent more likely than men to make referrals.[3] The same study also reveals that generally, women are more socially generous when it comes to sharing purchasing decisions as well as positive and negative consumer reviews. Being aware of *her* impact is the tip of the iceberg. You must also know her influence, which will only benefit your brand experience strategies so they resonate with the decision maker: the woman.

I define the brand experience (BX) as the sum of all interactions a customer has with a brand, across all phases of the customer life cycle, including how customers perceive these interactions. As you read through this book, you will see why a complete interactional brand experience is even more essential to the female consumer, and just how influential the female consumer is.

Yet the reality is, most businesses still don't take this huge female customer segment very seriously, and organizational team members are not given the tools to tailor the customer experience to women. In a very real, male-dominated world, women are still dealing with the long-standing idea of the perceived female lack of power when in fact she has been the main influencer of purchases for centuries.

Reaching female customers is made even more difficult by the fact that men make up 76 percent of C-suite level executives, 73 percent of senior vice presidents, 70 percent of vice presidents, and 65 percent of senior managers/directors, according to the most recent Women in the Workplace Survey.[4] This gap between who designs the female customer experience and the female buyer is enormous. The bottom line is that men create the brand experience for females—men who are physiologically different from these females. And the myriad females these male leaders aren't reaching? Well, women are said to control about $43 trillion a year in consumer spending.[5] That's why so many businesses are falling short in securing their biggest potential income source: women. What an oversight and loss that is.

Ninety-one percent of women still feel misunderstood by advertisers,[6] and according to Linkage Research's Entrepreneur Tracking Study, 76 percent of women question whether or not most companies even comprehend their needs.[7] For ages, it seems as if women have been preaching about the need for change, but what I have realized through my research, experiences, and conversations is that women are not the only ones who can bring about change. Men must join the movement. Men, especially in leadership positions, must be open to learning how to create experiences that speak to women; this includes not only female consumers and employees, but also their wives, daughters, mothers, family, and friends.

Imagine a new world where your company knows how to talk to women, to the world's most influential consumer, because you know their desires and needs, and can meet their expectations. Imagine a world where women fall in love with your brand and remain loyal to you. In this world, you would not only see an enormous increase in customer satisfaction (and profits), you would also be able to close the gap between what you want to achieve and how your team members go about achieving it. Imagine a brand experience that not only satisfies the world's most influential consumer, but builds trust, loyalty, and referrals.

The customer experience you offer is the number one differentiator between you and other brands. It's the key reason—even more than price and quality—that customers will choose *you* over your competitors.

Brand experience has been a buzz initiative for a few years now. Many successful organizations quickly figured out how to incorporate BX into the work they did, which has made it harder today for those who were not early adopters. Companies like Starbucks, Apple, Dropbox, Zappos, and Amazon have, over time, trained consumers to have high expectations of their entire buying experience, not just the actual transaction itself.

Consumers—especially women—want a tailored experience that speaks to them personally, from start to finish, and this has completely changed the marketplace. Customers today demand more and expect more, and companies, no matter the industry, are under pressure to keep up with the public's ever-increasing expectations. Not keeping up with the ever-increasing expectations of the female consumer will negatively affect an organization's ability to develop necessary relationships with their female consumers and form trust.

In my fifteen years of developing BX programs for organizations across North America and around the world, I've come to learn that businesses don't spend enough time understanding their customers in general. And via my firsthand car-buying experiences, extensive research, and professional experience, I know that male *and* female leaders in charge of brand management and cultivating the consumer experience are largely ignoring women—the most influential segment of buyers. Why is that? Considering that a woman has such purchasing influence, you would think it would be important to understand and deliver her needs, wants, and expectations.

If you want your organization or business to undergo real, sustainable change in regard to the experiences you provide to the female consumer, you must be willing to take a good, hard look at who women are and what makes us tick. Your organization needs a belief system and culture women can get behind, a shift in mindset, and a willingness to make changes to the core of your business—changes that speak to women as respected consumers. This is the type of business that appeals to women.

You hold the power to impact your customer's day with a single interaction. You have the ability to be the highlight of her day by taking the time to personalize the experience you provide, being compassionate and anticipatory. You'll knock the competition out of the water and gain ultimate power as a brand if you focus on the experience you provide to your female consumer.

This book will show you how to achieve these goals. I have researched the habits of female consumers and the impact women have on households, businesses, and the world's economy. I have used my own experiences to build upon this research and discover how to create a successful brand experience for women. Whether you are a woman or a man, as a business leader, you need this knowledge in order to transform the way you deliver a customer experience to your most important and influential consumers: women.

Before you read on, I leave you with one more thought: You always have a choice to make the consumer your priority. Every day before you open for business or walk into work, you have a choice to stand still or evolve. You have the choice to make the *female* consumer a priority. Only you stand in your way of capturing *her* dominant force in the economic world. You can stay where you are and continue doing what you're doing, or you can do something better. My goal is to show you how to take key steps forward, implement them in what you do, and be consistent in your choice to evolve. You will learn to understand your female consumer, journey through her eyes, and create the real relationships she craves; you will grasp the importance of hiring more women, and how to create consistency in the experience that will win her heart.

If you're ready to evolve as a leader, this book will give you the knowledge you need to understand the female consumer, create real relationships, and deliver "wow" moments that make you stand out above the rest, bringing your business into the top tier of the best BX organizations—those that have the ability to execute an experience that speaks to the female, to *her,* the decision maker.

In the chapters that follow, I'll share information on the evolution of women and their spending power, insights on the physiological differences between men and women, the scientific power of love and how it relates to your brand, why connection and accountability matter in reaching your female customer, how you can tailor the customer experience to the decision maker—the woman—and how to attract the elusive female consumer. Tip: It takes more than simply offering a pink version of your product.

This book is meant to be a quick read—to give you ideas and expand your mind in order to think bigger than the typical "customer experience." I want to help you Custom*Her* Experience.

My hope is also that you will be inspired to think a little differently, to do more than you thought possible, and transform the brand experience you offer the decision maker—the woman. And who knows? It might even strengthen the relationships you have with women in your own life!

——————— O N E ———————

THE EVOLUTION OF WOMEN AND
THEIR SPENDING POWER

———————————————

*B*efore I present to you *how* to tailor your brand experience toward women, I want to show you *why* you should. Why do women matter for your business, and how did they become the incredibly powerful purchasers they are today, especially when you remember those dark ages when women couldn't own property, controlled no finances, and had virtually no say politically?

For centuries/millennia, women have been spending influencers and decision makers . . . perhaps not always with their own pocket money, but with their persuasive roles in the family and society. Although for many, many years, this influence took place behind the scenes, at home, we are now entrenched in an era when women are established Chief Purchasing Officers with strong earning and spending power.

Even before women had their own money, property, and rights, their influence was felt heavily simply because they are the great communicators. Everyone in a woman's sphere was apt to hear about her experience with a product, *especially* if it was negative. Women love to talk and share their feelings, and they have been doing this since the beginning of time. They share the good, the bad, and the ugly with just about anyone who will listen; and now the whole world listens through a megaphone!

Let's take a look at the evolving role of the purchasing power of women throughout history to see how we arrived in this modern age of influential women with their own earning and buying power. And I'll show you just how formidable women are in today's consumer market.

WOMEN RULE

The rise of the female consumer's power and influence is reminiscent of a roller coaster's journey. The climb has always been slow, with a lot of opposing resistance. The success, unfortunately, is often short-lived before the fall comes at warp speed. Then, in the blink of an eye, the climb starts again. For women, this cycle dates back thousands of years. Unfortunately, the true influence of women has often been buried among ancient ruins.

In ancient Egypt, at least six women rose up as the highest decision makers in the land, not counting the dozens of others who acted as queen-regents or high priestesses or influential wives. Hatshepsut (r. 1479–1458 BCE) was the first female ruler of ancient Egypt to reign with the full authority of a pharaoh. Her name means "Foremost of Noble Women" or "She Is First Among Noble Women." She was the fifth pharaoh of the Eighteenth Dynasty and was regarded as one of the best Egyptian rulers. And talk about purchasing power: Hatshepsut was the richest female head of state in Egypt's history, says Kara Cooney, an Egyptologist at the University of California, Los Angeles.[1] As ruler of one of the largest realms in the ancient world, she also maintained control of substantial gold, copper, and precious stone mines, whose productivity would be worth about $2 billion today.[2]

The most well known of all female Egyptian rulers was Cleopatra VII, who began her rule in 51 BCE. She's remembered by Elizabeth Taylor fans for her great beauty and fiery relationships, but in reality, the real Cleopatra—as depicted in paintings and on coins of the time— was rather small and plain. Regardless of her true physical appearance, Cleopatra was educated, respected, and extremely commanding. In fact, when it came to monetary power, she led the charge. Authenticated monetary records collaborate that Cleopatra practiced the ancient tradition of writing discourses on weights and measures, as well as currency. She also improved Egypt's economy by making clear the fiduciary nature of the bronze coinage in circulation, the value of which was determined not by weight, but by Cleopatra. The result raised the value of Egyptian bronze currency to that of the Roman denarius, the coinage of choice at the time throughout the Western world.[3] Yes, this incredibly powerful woman single-handedly reformed and enhanced exponentially the financial status of her entire country. Some historians value her net worth as high as $95.8 billion.[4]

Egyptian women weren't alone in their influence. Throughout history, powerful female leaders have made their mark: Eleanor of Aquitaine (1122–1202), the Queen of England and of France; Mary Queen of Scots (1542–1587), who became the most influential female in Scotland as queen at only six days old; Victoria, Queen of England (1819–1901), whose reign, at the time, was the longest in English history; Tzu-Hsi, the Empress of China (1835–1908), who rose from concubine to influential ruler who modernized and reformed the government. The list goes on and on.

However, a female that reigned also controlled the men in her domain. As a result, there were many attempts by men to overthrow these female rulers. In fact, in certain instances, a female ruler would only be allowed to lead if she supported the male-dominated system that surrounded her. A notable exception was Catherine the Great, one of the world's great historical figures. Catherine the Great has been credited with modernizing Russia, bringing it into an age of modern enlightenment, and, among other accomplishments, giving girls a chance at an education by establishing the first state-funded school for young women.

Of course, a female's power and influence weren't always the result of authority over others or how much she was worth. There have been a multitude of other trailblazing women throughout history who were just as, if not more, influential than those formidable rulers. These women dared to be bold, living in their superpower, all the while redefining what a woman could achieve. Jane Austen, who defined an entire literary genre, and Maya Angelou, who spoke up about the prejudices she'd endured as a black woman, are examples of great leaders who didn't always have the matching pocketbooks.

One of the most impressive traits that all these women shared was the tenacity to break through glass ceilings, burst through walls, and challenge the status quo. These admirable queens, literary geniuses, and countless other women throughout history all believed in making the impossible possible, which has made them all remarkable figures. Each provides undeniable proof that women have always held stature, influence, and power, even if this influence is often buried in books, stories, and memories.

Today, however, surely we've progressed well past the point of relegating the influence of women to the back burner. Right?

Unfortunately, modern history shows that the world began to assign to women the role of homemaker and nothing else. Women couldn't vote, were discouraged from owning businesses, and struggled to make strides in an increasingly male-dominated world. The battle has been hard, but women keep fighting for equality; the war is ours to win.

Although female influence has slid in and out of darkness, there has always been one place women have ruled undetected: in their very own matriarchal society, the home. By definition, a matriarchy is a "family, group, or state governed by a matriarch (a woman who is head of a family or tribe)." Have you ever heard the saying, "The man is the head, but the woman is the neck"? This cheeky quotation perfectly depicts just how much influence a woman has within her matriarchal society. The man may be "the decision maker" and the face in society, but the woman turns his head in the direction she wants him to go.

While women throughout the ages may have lost the opportunity to rule a country or take a seat at the C-suite table, their power has always been a flame that has burnt brightly within the home. The reality is (and has always been) that women hold the most power, control, and influence within their communities and family.

YOU CAN'T KEEP A GOOD WOMAN DOWN

As women began to grow quietly as influencers behind the scenes, their opinions generally became more respected in the household. By 1910, women not only seemed to be turning the heads of their husbands, but those of advertisers and business owners (it helped that advertising agencies were beginning to hire a few women). Agencies and businesses started to recognize that women were the Chief Purchasing Officers for their families, deciding on food, household products, clothing, and appliances. As a result, advertisers began to feature women in print ads, on the radio, and on television.

Advertisers in the early 1900s would often represent young girls as picture-perfect versions of how their mothers and grandmothers were viewed in society. The goal was to "teach them young," molding young women and influencing their decisions/opinions about the products they would purchase in the future.

One of the biggest influences a mother has on her daughter centers on the concept of beauty, and advertisers played upon this, often using both mothers and daughters in ads, showing them performing skin and makeup routines together. Businesses and agencies sold their products with the goal that daughters would buy these same goods when they were ready to start their own beauty regimes. Even today, a mother will buy her daughter her first lip gloss or take her for her first facial. A mother will also decide such things as what shampoo her children use or which hairdresser they visit.

This shift in advertising back in the 1900s quietly showed the world how powerful the female influence was. Although most of the ads featured perfect-looking women smiling while performing a "woman's task," advertisers had begun to understand that if the ad was targeted well, other women would want to emulate the model featured in the ad and would therefore make the decision to purchase. Businesses and advertisers began to realize that once the product was in the home, the influence started. Each member of a woman's family—and even her friends—would be open to knowing why she had chosen that product, asking questions like "How does this work? Is this something I should consider buying? How much is it, and where can I purchase it?"

And so the Chief Purchasing Officer was born.

There was a direct parallel to the Chief Purchasing Officer title that advertisers gave to women and the rise of their influence in the professional world. By 1921, at the end of World War I, 17.7 percent of women aged fourteen and older were participating in the labor force.[5] Women suddenly had jobs that had previously been reserved solely for men—working in factories, in uniform overseas, as drivers, as radio operators, and in aircraft production. A surge of women entered the workforce throughout the war. Thirty-five thousand women served in uniform both at home and abroad. At the end of the war, women wanted to keep their jobs, but a patriarchal society and the men in their lives relegated them to a world within the home.

World War II marked a turning point for the female presence in the workforce. Women began to be seen not only as dutiful, loving wives and mothers; females were now contributing to the family financially. By 1970, women in the US represented 39.9 percent of the labor force, which increased the female impact on the economy.[6]

One thing, though, has never changed: Women have, do, and will continue to influence all household purchases. As the woman's presence has grown in the workplace, her influence has become stronger, more defined, and more empowered. Unfortunately, even with progress, women still represent only 21 percent of C-suite-level executives, leaving a majority of brand experiences to be designed by men, for men. Yet it is the woman who holds an 80–90 percent influence over all household purchases.[7]

It is the woman who is the decision maker.

MS. INDEPENDENT

Power is influence, and the female consumer is the most influential, making her the most powerful consumer. Over the past century, the female consumer has evolved from the "keeper of the house" to the Chief Purchasing Officer, and along the way she has been deemed the world's most influential consumer. A woman's spending power has grown exponentially as well (and much more quickly than her rise to the top of the corporate ladder).

In mid-December 2019, I boarded a (very) early flight to Fort Lauderdale, Florida. I was on my way to speak at an automotive conference on this very topic. As usual, I started chatting with my seatmate (an older woman), who asked me about my life, what I do for a living, my kids, and how I was able to travel the world and still be a mom. Mid-sentence, from the corner of my eye, I noticed a flash of the most intense pinkish/red color outside the window of the plane. I turned my head to see the sunrise illuminating the sky. The lights of the city below twinkled in the fading darkness, making the intensity of the sunrise even more beautiful.

I nodded out the window with a smile and said to the lovely woman, "The world is incredibly vast. There are so many opportunities to design your life."

She smiled back at me with a concerned look in her eyes.

"What?" I asked.

"It's so much easier for you today, as a woman, to see the world this way." She paused. "When I was growing up, the woman cared for the man. She kept the home. She tended to the children. A woman's world was her home." She took a deep breath and sighed. "There has been such an evolution. Women today make money, they make bold choices, and they most definitely steer their own ship."

She was exactly right. Of course, I'd never lived as a woman in the role to which society had assigned a woman. I sat quietly in appreciation for the path women before me had paved, so that today we can assert our independence. Women are finally influential in our own right. We are making more money because of our desire to work outside the home. With money comes power, and power is influence. Women are now able to influence as individuals, as their role continues to evolve from the more traditional "homemaker" to a "nontraditional professional." I came across an interesting experimental study that had the goal of identifying the different decisions women made based on their social role in society. The study revealed that women in "nontraditional professional" roles were making financial decisions, focusing on their own needs, and making bigger purchases without consultation.[8] Women will continue to attain more nontraditional roles, becoming not only the world's most influential consumers, but big contributors to the world's society.

Women now earn more college degrees than men and as of 2018, owned 12.3 million businesses in the US. (By comparison, there were only 402,000 women-owned businesses in 1972.) These businesses employ 9.2 million people and generate $1.8 trillion in revenue.[9] Although we need more women-owned businesses as a whole, it's heartening to see that some of the most powerful executives in business are now women. Women like Sheryl Sandberg, who, after four years as Facebook's Chief Operating Officer (COO), led the company through a highly criticized $100 billion IPO; Indra Nooyi, former Chief Executive Officer (CEO) and chair of PepsiCo and one of the top twenty of the world's one hundred most powerful women; and Mary Barra, chair and CEO of General Motors and the first female head of an automobile manufacturer.

There is still a lot of work to be done in promoting and sponsoring women to the top, as I will discuss in Chapter 7, however, I feel it is important to mention the influence women are finally making in a big way. As society evolves, women will continue to rise, and the decisions they make will impact your business. Consequently, earning her business is a sure path to financial success.

As the women of the world assert their independence, gaining confidence and seats at the table, female influence only intensifies.

Here are some facts that are hard to argue:

- According to a *Harvard Business Review* article, women hold a 94 percent influence over all home-furnishing purchases and a 92 percent influence over all vacation decisions. [10]

- Eighty-four percent of women are the sole preparer of meals in the household, with 61 percent stating that they prepare meals at least five times per week.[11] Therefore, females are buying the groceries and deciding on the brands they will present at the kitchen table.

- Women make 90 percent of household health-care decisions, which includes choosing the medical professionals the family uses, the form of care they feel comfortable with, and the medications they take. This also greatly impacts the type of insurance coverage the woman believes is right for her and her family[12] and accounts for 93 percent of over-the-counter pharmaceutical purchases.[13]

- Female gamers—yes, gamers—over the age of fifty-five spend more time online gaming than males aged fifteen to twenty-four,[14] and in 61 percent of all consumer electronics purchases, a woman either initiated the purchase or was involved in the purchase process.[15]

The female influence doesn't stop there! Women have major power in typically male-dominated sports as well. A female sports fan will bring people together to celebrate around her favorite events. This translates to increased grocery sales, beverage sales, memorabilia purchases, and influences where all of these purchases are made.

Women make up—

- 47.2 percent of Major League Soccer (MLS) fans

- 46.5 percent of MLB fans

- 43.2 percent of NFL fans

- 40.8 percent of NHL fans

- 37 percent of NBA fans

- and buy 46 percent of all official NFL merchandise![16]

A woman's purchasing power dominates the sports world. She holds the veto vote on ticket and merchandising purchases. The sports industry is no longer a man's world. Women look at sporting events as an opportunity to bring people together, create memories, and share in experiences. A woman is your most influential fan.

In finance, 93 percent of women say they have significant influence on what financial services their family needs.[17] Women influence where the family banks, where the kids will open their first savings accounts, and how the couple invests.

Last but not least, in one of the world's most male-dominated industries—automotive—female consumers are taking over and are here to stay. Women make up 65 percent of new car purchasers[18] and influence 85 percent of all vehicle purchases when in a coupled relationship.[19]

I'll say it again: Women are the world's economy, controlling about $20 trillion in worldwide spending.[20] After millennia, female independence is finally here to stay and grow. The question now becomes: are you equipped to capture and keep the attention of the world's most influential consumer?

THE FEMALE POWER PROBLEM

So what's the problem? Women are huge influencers—the Chief Purchasing Officers—so why don't companies simply reach out to them directly and effectively?

The fact is that companies are *still* not ready for this consumer group. Even worse, women feel misunderstood by most brands, even though women have quietly been gaining momentum regarding the influence they have on the world's economy. The reality is, many companies are unprepared. It is vital that they look in the accountability mirror and realize this. They don't have the tools their team members need to tailor the experience to a woman in order to drive her loyalty and referrals.

This problem dates to the early 1900s, when advertisers started to pay attention to the influence wives and mothers had on the consumption in households; unfortunately, the advertisements of this period painted a completely different picture than that of the reality. Advertisements still portrayed wives deferring to husbands in financial and child-rearing matters, when in reality it was the woman that made all of those decisions behind closed doors. What a missed opportunity for organizations to capitalize on the female influence.

A huge reason for the problem that existed back then still exists today. Men have always ruled the executive teams that design these advertisements. How could these men possibly understand how to market or sell to women, when most of them didn't understand or want to try to understand women? A majority lived under assumptions and didn't look to the women around them to change this portrait. And we all know what assuming does. It makes an ass out of you and me!

Marketers and executives today *think* they know what women want, need, desire, and dream about, but they're usually not coming close to hitting the mark. Of course, if you're in a company that has women at the top, you have a better chance at succeeding at this goal. Yet as I mentioned before, 85 percent of the world's executives are men, and only 3 percent of creative directors in marketing firms are women.

The tech industry is one of the fastest-growing industries today but still represents much larger male employment than female. The ten largest companies in Silicon Valley have 70 percent male employees, and in the top managerial and executive positions, the number of male employees rises to 83 percent.[21]

As a result, men ultimately create the brand experience; designed by men, for men. And in male-dominated industries like automotive and tech, it is taken one step further: The experience is not only designed by men and for men, but male field teams deliver the experience as well. Yet women account for 85 percent of *all* consumer purchases.[22] The gap between who buys and who designs the female consumer experience is *enormous*.

MARKETING TO WOMEN FAILS

History is full of feeble and ill-advised attempts by organizations to seemingly morph products into "women's products." Dell is a great example. In 2009, it tried to sell pink laptops from a new "Della" section of its website.[23] Women were outraged, and it took less than a week for Dell to remove the failed attempt at a "female-focused" site. A female consumer and a director of information technology (IT) posted: "As a female IT person, both at work and seemingly to the entire community some days, and a loyal Dell user, I am sorely aggrieved that Dell chose to give birth to 'Della.' Another male (I hope) engineered conception gone awry. This child can be thrown out with the bathwater." Myriad comments like these were the reason Dell made the choice to change the site so quickly.

Bic released its infamous "For Her" line of ballpoint pens in 2012 that made women everywhere wonder how they'd been able to survive using men's pens for so long. Not only did these "she-pens" insult women, but men felt awkward using them. Feedback from dissatisfied female customers included sarcastic comments such as, "I bought [this pen] for a woman at work, as she couldn't figure out how to use a man's pen. After I helped her open the package, she was super happy! She can now write in great pink and purple!" Another customer wrote, "I gave these to the men in my office and they all received pay cuts a few weeks later! Thanks, Bic, for helping me to bridge the pay gap."[24]

This bad press comes from a lack of understanding during the product development stage. What happened to Bic and Dell is what happens when you try to build your brand by looking at it through the lens of data rather than from the perspective of your female consumer.

Another marketing-to-women failure lies with US-based IBM. IBM defiantly set their eyes on transforming the misunderstandings of women in industries like technology, science, engineering, and mathematics through their "hack a dryer" campaign.[25] This campaign showed women in different scenarios holding hair dryers with confused looks on their faces, as if they were trying to contemplate what in the world to do with this high-tech appliance. The ad went on to show all the different (very female) things you can do with the parts of a hair dryer. The goal, I presume, was to inspire women to think bigger; that they can do anything with anything! Unfortunately, this message backfired. The responses from women, especially within the science and engineering industries, were less than stellar. There were thousands of tweets criticizing the campaign, calling it sexist, patronizing, and reinforcing of gender stereotypes. IBM has since apologized for "missing the mark" and removed the video.

Dove has had quite a few wins with their positive body image "Real Beauty" campaign, which features real women and empowers female consumers to see themselves in a positive light.[26] Unfortunately, their next campaign, released in England, featured limited-edition packaging representing abstract, shapeless soap bottles, which were supposed to represent diverse female body types. In theory, this has a positive implication. However, Dove only released seven different shapes, constraining women to choose the package that matched their shape, which increased self-consciousness. Many women weren't represented. This sent the wrong message. The campaign became a source of genuine concern on social platforms like Twitter and Facebook.

The food and beverage industries have had some major fails as well, when trying to market to women using a stereotypical approach. BrewDog released a special edition "BrewDog Pink IPA" on International Women's Day that tried to raise awareness for the gender pay gap. They even sold this Pink IPA for 20 percent less to those who identified as a woman.[27] Unfortunately, the criticism the campaign received outweighed the charitable efforts. One customer responded on Twitter with: "I'm so tired of brands doing lazy stunts in the name of equality and then when it falls flat trotting out the old 'oh nooo, we were using irony! We're good!'" A woman on BrewDog's Facebook page poked fun at the brand as well: "Let's show that 'enough is enough with stereotypes' by using a stereotype," adding the crying laughter and face palm emojis. "Sounds like trying to reel in a bad marketing decision." By way of explanation, BrewDog's head of global marketing, Sarah Warman, said in a statement to *Business Insider*, "Pink IPA is clearly an over-the-top ridiculing of the types of sexist marketing we often see from brands trying to engage a female audience." Even one of BrewDog's female leaders saw that this campaign didn't achieve what they set out to achieve. However, the tweets and comments bashing this attempt at marketing to women made it clear that consumers felt that BrewDog's lurid pink packaging and stereotypical "Pink IPA" brand name were a "send-up of the lazy marketing efforts targeting the female market."[28]

In another example, there was even an app designed to provide drinks offers from participating bars to subscribers. The app offered gender-specific drinks, splitting the options within the app according to gender, using stereotypical colors and types of drinks as the differentiator of the two sexes. For the men, the home screen was blue with offers for drinks such as beer and whisky. For women, it was pink, prosecco, and vodka drinks. Do drinks really need to be defined by sex? Women didn't think so and they didn't like being called out in that way.

The last thing women want is to have something made especially for us because companies feel women won't be able to handle an item in its original "male" form, color, or design. Especially if the result is pink. Women hate being patronized, and we do not like being singled out. We work just as hard and do many of, if not all, the same tasks as men. Instead, view and treat women as the competent people we are. Using the color pink or other stereotypically female ideas as the basis for a campaign means there is a high chance you will push your most influential customers away rather than bringing them closer to your brand.

Those are just a few examples of how misunderstood the female consumer is. All businesses, especially male-dominated ones, need to step into the twenty-first century and start providing an experience that their female consumer wants and deserves.

Remember, the business you run is not a product business; it is a people business. Exceptional user experiences win every time, and you can't provide those experiences without truly understanding the female consumer. Without your loyal customers and their referrals, you wouldn't have a consistent flow of new customers. Your female consumers will deliver on this for you if you take the time to design an experience that breaks the script, is consistent, and is genuine.

If you are an organization where a male presence dominates your executive team, it is essential that you open your eyes to effective branding for women. We are at a time when the roles and power of women have evolved, and brand experiences must also evolve with them for companies to thrive. This book will provide you with the effective tools to tap into the powerful Chief Purchasing Officer's psyche and pocketbook. Now let's take a look at how women are inherently different than men, and why this matters to your brand.

TWO

BIOLOGY MEETS BRANDING

There are behavioral differences between men and women, and as a result, their expectations about interacting with a brand also differ. Women think differently, act differently, solve problems differently, and are much more emotionally driven than men. These distinctions can be scientifically linked to the physiological differences between men and women. It simply comes down to biology.

Women are not the same as men. You know this and I know this, but it's amazing how often company leaders forget this when it comes to branding. Male and female differences originate at the cellular and molecular levels. The notion that men are from Mars and women are from Venus is true in so many regards! We are physiologically built differently, which means our ideas of what makes an experience worth talking about are also very different.

Many of these variations between men and women—from communication style to connectivity in relationships to depth of emotions—are because of fundamental disparities in our brains. If you learn what these are and why you should pay attention to them, women will flock to the brand experiences that are tailored to their brain waves.

THE GREAT COMMUNICATORS

Women are master communicators. The connection a woman makes and the relationships she has built through the many stories she shares are vital to a woman feeling heard and validated. That's because women use both sides of their brains to communicate, while men only use one. This gives women a distinct advantage.

According to Sahab Uddin, MD, the features of left and right hemispheres vary considerably in men and women.[1] Men have verbal centers on only the left hemisphere, while women have verbal centers on both hemispheres. Therefore, when conversing or explaining feelings, a person, place, or story, an incident, or any object, females use more words to communicate. In fact, higher amounts of a language protein exist in women, and as a result, they use more words daily—20,000 versus 13,000 for men.[2] Fewer verbal centers in males means fewer connections between men's feelings or memories and their word centers. Additionally, it has been found that women have the advantage of being able to express their emotions and feelings more than men—and take more interest in doing so—due to their increased amount of verbal centers.

Communication is a huge reason why women yield such power in the marketplace. Think about this for a quick second. If you're a woman reading this right now, can you recall a time when you had a great experience or life event and shared it with your girlfriends? Overwhelmingly, that answer is "of course!" We love to talk about what happens in our day, often at length. Now, think of a time when you had a negative experience or when something went wrong; don't you sometimes reveal how that made you feel and share that story on an even greater scale, sharing all the gory details? Again, "yes" is the obvious answer. Women are naturally built to do that! Our brains are wired that way. We will go on and on for days about how the experience made us feel. If the female consumer loves your brand, they will refer you. If they are unsatisfied, they will let the whole world know. Their many verbal centers compel them!

Women not only influence the purchases made by their partner and themselves, they also influence three to four generations—their parents, children, and extended families. Women are both buyers and influencers. They both purchase the products they need for themselves and influence the spending of the generations that surround them.

No matter the century, whether women have their own earning power or not, they have always been brilliant communicators. Women are built this way—it's biological! Whether it was talking at quilting bees, relaying their opinions to family, or sharing gossip over the fence, women took pleasure in sharing their experiences. Well before social media even existed, women cultivated a social world through communication with anyone who would listen.

WOMEN TODAY *and* SOCIAL MEDIA

Women love to talk and share their feelings and have been doing this since the beginning of time. Not only do women use social media to vet products and analyze brands, but they use social

continued

27

media as a platform for sharing and discussing their feelings. Women lean on their social platforms for advice and acceptance, and have taken over the social world as we know it. They will share the good, the bad, and the ugly with just about anyone who will listen; and now the whole world listens to her opinions that are amplified on a whole new level! On average, women will mention brands 73 times per week. The question becomes whether or not the story they tell alongside the mention of the brand is a positive or negative one.[3] Unfortunately for companies, a more powerful message is when a woman has disappointing experiences. Negative stories are often spread far more quickly and widely than those that are positive.

In the modern age of social media, the rise of women's purchasing power has reached an all-time high. Women still have the passion and ability to help grow and support a brand or bring it down by word of mouth—now through the incredibly powerful method of social media. The female Chief Purchasing Officer takes this responsibility very seriously. Now, the whole world listens to what women have to say. In today's society, women actively use social media to share what's happening in their lives with new connections, friends, colleagues, and family. Men, on the other hand, tend to use social media to gather information about a topic of interest, not to share about life's experiences. It's a different way of engaging. A 2012 Nielsen study showed that women spend 30 percent more time every day networking through the mobile web, or through apps, than their male counterparts.[4]

Here's another question for you: Do you want to control social awareness that is brought to your brand? I am hoping you said "yes"; the decision maker can help you do this. You just have to give her a reason to shout positive stories from the mountaintops. The experience you provide to her will give her the nudge she needs to engage the myriad verbal centers in her brain. She can make or break your brand through her innate need for strong communication. A female holds this power, and she knows it.

THE SCIENCE OF FEMALE BONDING

When women feel a sense of connection with something or someone, the hormone oxytocin is released. Oxytocin comes into play at high concentrations during positive social interactions such as falling in love, experiencing an orgasm, or for women, giving birth and breastfeeding.

Many people often refer to oxytocin as the bonding hormone. Sharing confidences or emotions, and creating relationships and connections activates the pleasure center in a woman's brain, facilitating her ability to identify kinship. However, researchers have found that in men, this same hormone improves a man's ability to identify competitive relationships.[5] An intriguing difference between the sexes.

Women pride themselves on the successful relationships they have and keep, especially those friendships with our besties! These friendships provide women with an outlet to share their problems, concerns, and happy moments in their lives. Most of our emotional and mental strength comes from the deep bonds we hold with our girlfriends. There's that oxytocin driving us again!

A quote from Beyoncé comes to mind that displays just how important relationships are to women: "I love my husband, but it is nothing like a conversation with a woman that understands you. I grow so much from those conversations."

I have one childhood friend I have known since I was four years old. In third grade, we would run around the schoolyard and hide out under the monkey bars. We would talk about everything and nothing, then skip back into school. Thirty years later, we still have conversations that last for hours, not realizing where the time has gone. The really special thing about deep relationships is that it doesn't matter how much time has passed; friends and loved ones can pick up as if it were yesterday.

Because women innately and biologically put more emphasis on relationships in their lives, they often, sometimes to a fault, expect others to value equally the importance of creating relationships. Which makes how you create and keep the relationships you have with the women in your life—whether at home, at work, or with your customers—extremely important. The bonds you form impact the decision your female customer makes on whether or not she chooses to do business with you.

Your brand is built on relationships. The connection you have with your female consumers—the bond—how you deliver an experience, and the way you market to them will dictate the relationship women will have with your company.

Unfortunately for female consumers, many of the men who are industry leaders cannot physiologically and naturally connect with women in the way a woman would expect. Many men in leadership positions find incredible success because of traits such as competitiveness, dominance, and independence, which is in direct opposition to what most women biologically value. Therefore, many of the men making branding decisions for women don't understand why it is so important for women to share confidences and emotions, or spend the time getting to know someone—the building blocks that form and strengthen relationships.

Whether they "get it" or not, men in leadership positions must accept that relationships are incredibly important to women. Our female brains dictate this. Only by accepting this scientific fact will leaders be able to create positive connections between women and their brands.

THE LIMBIC BRAIN

Hormones aren't the only difference when it comes to men and women. The limbic system is the emotional and memory hub of our brains. It is responsible for motivation, emotion, learning, and long-term memory.

Some research shows that women have a larger deep limbic system than males do.[6] Having a larger deep limbic system could be the reason many women are more in touch with their emotions and feelings, and are often better at expressing these sentiments than men. We make many decisions based on our feelings, and a woman's limbic brain is larger than that of a man, making the feelings she has toward an experience even more influential. The limbic system is responsible for processing emotions and for human behavior and decision making, which is why businesses need to create more connected and relationship-focused experiences for the female consumer's larger deep limbic system.

Her hippocampus, which is responsible for long-term memory creation, is also larger than a male's hippocampus. So if you ever wonder why a woman in your life can remember a disagreement in minute detail five years later, blame the hippocampus! If you want to create loyalty with your female consumers, you want her to have fond, long-lasting memories about your brand and the experiences you provide to her.

It boils down to this: I've observed that women seem to innately value connection, communication, and feelings more than men. We can't fight biology! As a result, female consumers want a relationship with your brand, and they need to be able to communicate how they're feeling and what they want and expect.

If you want to drive customer satisfaction with your Chief Purchasing Officer—the woman—you must accept the distinctive, fundamental differences between men and women. Only when you recognize these differences will you be able to reach this consumer group effectively. It is to your advantage to pay attention to how you make a woman feel and the experience you provide to her; doing this is a leap forward in providing the decision maker with a positive experience that meets her expectations and leaves her feeling good. It's not rocket science; it's simple physiology.

THREE

MAKING HER FALL IN LOVE WITH YOUR BRAND EXPERIENCE

*D*o you remember the first time you fell in love?

I do. I was fifteen years old and head over heels for a hunky high school hockey player (I am Canadian, and hockey players are a *big* deal). Every time he would walk around the corner of our school hallway, I would feel butterflies in my stomach, my palms would get sweaty, and I would have goose bumps all over my body.

I'm sure you've felt the same way at some point in your life (at least I hope so!). Did you know that the same chemicals that cause all of these reactions when we fall in love are also present when a woman goes shopping? In other words, a woman experiences the same incredible feelings she gets swooning over a crush as she does while finding the perfect little black dress or purchasing a car that meets all her criteria. Women are falling in love when they shop for your brand! In return, your business must earn their loyalty and trust, and avoid disappointing them, so that you can keep the relationship strong and long.

THE SCIENTIFIC POWER OF LOVE

Let me lead you through the journey of falling in love. "Love" may not be the most popular word in organizations, especially male-dominated organizations. But the truth is, how the female consumer feels decides everything, and the only differentiators you have between you and your competitors are your people and the experience they provide. The Gallup organization says, "If you do not make an emotional connection with customers, then satisfaction is worthless."[1]

If you want to be a women-centric business, you want women to fall in love with and emotionally attach themselves to your brand. When women shop with you, they go on a journey, and if they interact with you in a positive way, there are three chemicals that are discharged. These are dopamine, serotonin, and oxytocin—three of the same chemicals that are released when you fall in love with someone!

1. **DOPAMINE**—According to Harvard University, dopamine is a chemical produced by a person's brain that plays a starring role in motivating their behavior.[2] It is released when we take a bite of delicious food, when we have sex, after we exercise, and most important to our discussion, when we have successful social interactions. In an evolutionary context, dopamine rewards us for beneficial behaviors and motivates us to repeat them. When your brand experience focuses on the interaction a female consumer has with you, dopamine is released in her brain. This chemical release leads to her

desire to repeat these repetitive interactions with your brand. So shopping is, indeed, addictive.

2. **SEROTONIN**—Serotonin is also known as the "happiness chemical" and plays a role in how a person feels about things. Creating an experience that stimulates happy feelings will, in turn, stimulate the release of serotonin. The goal here is to send a woman on a journey filled with positive stimuli. This way, she feels happy throughout her experience with your brand.

3. **OXYTOCIN**—As I mentioned in the previous chapter, oxytocin is the bonding hormone, which makes women crave connections. It is released when a person is shopping, in the same way as when they are falling in love. Again, this hormone affects women more rigorously than it affects men, which is why women want to connect with your brand. As a result, when you take the brand experience you offer one step further and create a relationship with your female consumers, you are entering a bonding zone. Once a woman has bonded with your brand, she is bound to be fiercely loyal. Although poets and authors have tried to describe love, in the world of neuroscience, researchers have found that the naturally occurring hormone oxytocin and love are intimately related. Often called the love drug, oxytocin plays a role in bonding, maternal instinct, enduring friendship, marriage, and orgasms. Loretta Graziano Breuning, PhD, professor emerita at California State University, says that oxytocin is a mingling of trust and physical touch, as well as lovemaking. A key component to earning her business is developing that trust, which leads to the release of oxytocin—helping her to fall in love with your brand and its people.[3]

If you want to build a love connection with your female consumer, your goal is to stimulate the release of these chemicals. After all, who can fight biology?

IT'S ABOUT THE CHASE!

I am going to let you in on a little secret: It's not about the product a woman buys. It's about the journey she takes when she interacts with your brand. It is the *chase* she enjoys! It is about the little moments when she connects with your brand and creates a relationship with you that dictates whether or not she'll choose to do business with you again. See, the body's neurotransmitters, which conduct impulses across a synapse, surge when a consumer is considering buying something new. A woman connects not only with the product but also with the experiences leading up to the purchase.

Interestingly, our brains play a massive role in how we feel before we decide to make a purchase. As I mentioned earlier, not only is the woman's limbic brain double the size of a man's, the release of hormones impacts how she feels even after the purchase.

Your brain actually calculates how buying an object of desire will feel before you consciously decide whether or not to purchase it. Even though you can't see inside a woman's brain, you can go all-in on the notion that it is the journey before the purchase that is the most intense and important aspect of the purchase for her.

Women tend to go out for some "retail therapy" when they are having a bad day or feeling out of sorts. I know this is something that is made fun of in movies and books, but there is truth to it. Women can feel better when they journey through a mall, receiving little hits of dopamine and releases of serotonin, which could turn a not-so-great day into a better one (until she gets her credit card bill, that is!).

In a study conducted in 2007, neuroscientists scanned both men's and women's brains as the subjects considered a range of products. The scientists noted that the nucleus accumbens—aka the pleasure center— showed more activity during the journey of the purchase rather than when making the purchase itself.[4] The pleasure centers in men and women are stimulated and heightened for different reasons. Both men and women enjoy the journey, but a woman craves the connection with the person she's interacting with and the mood or atmosphere that's been created. A man responds best to the physical product for which he's shopping. This makes the experience the woman has when shopping with you of high importance.

If anybody knows me, they know I *love* shoes with a capital *L!* I love the hunt for the perfect shoe even more than the purchase of the now 367 pairs I have in my possession. Each pair of shoes I have bought comes with a story about the hunt: walking into the store, looking around, smelling the new leather, having a sales associate sit me down while he or she runs into the back to find my size, receiving the story of where the shoe was made and how it was manufactured. Even having the shoe slipped onto my foot is something I find exhilarating!

I was recently shopping at an outlet store in Fort Lauderdale, Florida. It was late on a Thursday evening. The hunt was on with only an hour until the store closed. I walked into the store and was greeted by aisles and aisles of designer shoes. With my right shoe in my hand, I scanned my sizes and slipped on shoe after shoe, placing each beautifully crafted pair in my basket. Then I heard the announcement that the store would be closing in fifteen minutes. I gasped, scurrying to see the last row of shoes and then dashing over to the counter. A half hour and six pairs later, I was happily skipping to my car. I got on the phone (and Instastories) almost immediately to share the experience I'd just had—oh, and photos of my new shoes!

When I got home, I lined up all my new shoes in my closet and went on with my night. And while I love the shoes I purchased, I still can't help but smile, thinking about the journey I took to find those shoes. It wasn't just about the shoes. My entire shopping experience had ignited my pleasure center, and I am still feeling the effects.

New count: 373 pairs of shoes.

Most of your female consumers go through the same emotional journey. Women, regardless of the season or the state of the economy, seem drawn to shopping and how it makes them feel. The question is whether or not you will capitalize on gaining an emotional connection with her.

Women react to anticipation, excitement, and the release of dopamine. It is the "foreplay"—the anticipation and experience—your brand provides a woman before she even purchases that excites her. Shopping is an experience that fills an emotional function, and most often, female consumers seek arousal and enjoyment from the shopping journey.

It is my belief that brands can learn from the impact that retail therapy has on their female consumers. If you can design an experience that will build anticipation and excitement, and forge a connection with your female consumer, you will guide her on a journey during which she will enjoy the chase, making it a no-brainer for her to say yes to the purchase. Women will experience serious hits of dopamine and serotonin if you spend time curating an experience that speaks to her needs, wants, and desires. Doing this will get you and your team much closer to meeting her expectations.

As one domino falls onto the next, she will also start to create a bond with your brand and possibly fall in love. Examining the journey your female consumer takes with your brand and tweaking it to include all the little moments that make her fall in love with your product or service are in your best interest. These small moments lead to a female consumer's love affair with your brand, which will turn her into a brand ambassador for you. Your female customers will give you their loyalty, make referrals for you, and be customers for life.

If you can cultivate these feelings of falling love in a female customer throughout the journey she takes with your brand, you will win every time.

THE TRUST ACCOUNT

Trust is the foundation of all good relationships and is very important to the female consumer. Women pride themselves on the relationships they have and keep. In a study called "Trust and Gender: An Examination of Behavior, Biases, and Beliefs," it was found that men trust more than women, and women are more trustworthy than men.[5] The trust the female consumer has with your brand reflects her belief in the honesty, transparency, and positive intentions your brand has.

According to Dr. Breuning, "Trust is the authentic feeling you have in the presence of a person whom your body senses is safe. That is a good feeling that stimulates oxytocin. When trust is not authentic, your body might give you a message to be careful around that person."[6] Without trust, customers, especially females, will not buy from you, refer you, or be loyal to you.

The foundation of any relationship is trust, and that applies in every way to your business relationships. Research shows that companies with high trust levels outperform companies with low trust levels by 186 percent.[7] If your customers don't trust you, you won't be able to retain them; if you aren't able to retain them, you definitely don't have their loyalty. But when your brand is trusted by its consumers, notably females, those customers are willing to pay more, come back to do business with you again, and tell others about their experience with you.

In every interaction you have with a customer, you increase or decrease trust. In these moments, you also gain the opportunity to change and positively shape their perception of you, your team members, and your brand. Retention and loyalty not only drive top-line sales but also reduce turnover.

Fostering emotional connections that lead to meaningful relationships often gets dismissed because it takes effort and requires a caring nature. What we think or feel when serving a customer doesn't really matter. Standing in your customer's shoes (especially the female customer) and caring enough about them as a person is really the delta that pivots the experience your brand and team provide. Have you heard the saying, "In business, it's not what you know, but who you know and who knows you"? No one will stick their neck out for anyone they don't have a real relationship with, your customers included. They won't shout their praises unless they feel cared for. I can testify to this as an entrepreneur. My business is built on referrals, and those referrals come from companies with which I have created long-standing relationships.

So why do businesses have such a hard time creating connections with their female consumers?

Building trust with your female consumer base is essential when it comes to referrals and their desire to purchase. The female has to feel good about a situation to move forward with just about anything. The popular author and speaker Simon Sinek states that the consumer makes decisions based off of emotions, and he is right, especially in regard to the female consumer.

I believe you have a zero-balance trust account with every customer in the beginning of a business relationship, and your business can make or break this trust in the moments it interacts with the female customer. It's up to you whether or not you make deposits in her trust account or let it go into overdraft. Every time you connect with a customer, you have an opportunity to pay into her trust account, helping you to uncover what your female customer wants or needs. A huge part of earning her business is being able to earn her trust. The trust a female consumer has in your brand yields a stronger relationship, which leads to her sharing her needs and wants more openly with your brand or its associates. This will make your business a powerful force. You will then be delivering an experience that is just right for her. This is critical to recognize because if you don't put positive deposits into her trust account, and you have a service failure or her expectations are not met, you will have a very hard time regaining her trust.

You and your team *will* drop the ball (you are only human, after all!), and without a positive balance of positive experiences in her trust account, you will go into overdraft. Studies show that it takes twelve positive interactions to make up for one negative one.[8] You can see now how hard you will have to work to get out of the overdraft situation.

You hold that power, through the experience you provide a woman, to earn and keep her trust account in a positive balance. This, however, takes hard work and consistency.

LOYALTY

In lasting relationships, loyalty is key. Acquiring a new customer can cost five times more than retaining an existing customer. Increasing customer retention by 5 percent can increase profits from 25 to 95 percent. The success rate of selling to a customer you already have is 60 to 70 percent, while the success rate of selling to a new customer is 5 to 20 percent.[9] That's why earning your customer's loyalty is key to your business's success.

While it may seem like no big deal to "drop the ball" or not meet your customer's expectations, we all know that once this happens, a seed is laid for bad habits. It is smart business to be consistent and pay attention to what matters: your customers and the experience you provide to them. If not, your business is on the way to losing a loyal customer.

Loyalty is huge when you're in a healthy relationship. All of us can attest to that. To that end, I want you to jot down two or three companies that have gained your trust, and therefore, your loyalty. Then, right next to these companies, write down why you are loyal to them. After that, write down how they make you feel.

COMPANY	WHY	HOW DID THEY MAKE YOU FEEL?

Look at the reasons why these companies have made it into your top three. Sure, they may offer you convenience (like Amazon) but what I guarantee you have also listed is consistency, trust, ease of doing business, and accountability (when something goes wrong, they make it right). Price may have made it in there, but it's less likely. Now look at the "How did they make you feel?" column. Do you have things listed like "happy," "special," "important," or "excited"? All of these emotions lead to trust, relationships, and ultimately, the journey of "falling in love" with a brand, which earns loyalty.

There is a fun little family restaurant that my family and I frequent. Having three kids with varying levels of taste buds and a nut allergy, I find it a challenge to choose a restaurant that we all like. La Veranda is that restaurant for us. It has a great wine list (best in the area), doesn't use nuts in any of its food, and makes the best pizza (that all my kids like!). The waiters remember our names, treat the kids like little adults, and keep them occupied, so Mom and Dad can actually enjoy a dinner in relative peace. When I ask where the kids want to go for dinner, La Veranda is almost always the answer. If they had only provided this positive experience once or twice but then failed, we might give them one more chance, but that would be it. However, they haven't dropped the ball yet and the consistent, positive experience keeps bringing us back. I have referred friends to them and even brought my grandparents there for our Friday dinners.

It doesn't take complicated programs or processes to create an experience that your customers come back for. Actually, it is quite simple. The hard work is in keeping your genuine and personalized experience consistent, so you are putting more in your customers' trust account than what you are taking out. This increases customer loyalty.

DISAPPOINTMENT: BROKEN HEARTS AND FAILED EXPECTATIONS

With every great love story comes the risk of a broken heart. Though you may cultivate the feeling of love with your female consumers, it is the consistency with which you live up to their expectations that will keep them interested. No one wants a partner who starts out as a wonderful person and then lets you down time and time again. Same goes for a brand.

Disappointment is simply experiencing unfilled hopes and expectations that are not met, and it is said to greatly impact decision making. According to a 2010 study on decision making, individuals tend to modify their behavior in an often unpredictable way just to avoid experiencing negative emotions.[10]

Any disappointment your female customer may feel when doing business with you has an effect on the decision she may make to do business with you in the future. When you don't meet the Chief Purchasing Officer's expectations consistently, she will find herself feeling the negative emotion of disappointment, which leads to a lack of trust that could lead to a brand breakup.

In author Amanda Lovelace's compelling book of poetry *The Princess Saves Herself in This One* (Kansas City, MO: Andrews McMeel, 2017), a queen offers a cube of sugar to the narrator of the poem, who places it on her tongue only to discover that it is salt. The poem reads, "That is what abuse is: Knowing you are going to get salt but still hoping for sugar for nineteen years."

We abuse our customers all the time. We do this by promising them a consistent, personal, and genuine experience, and instead we hand them salt (when we get too tired or an employee feels "off" one day). Unlike the poet (who only has one mother), your customers have choices, and if we don't give them a consistent experience, they will stop choosing you.

For instance, I travel a lot. I call an airplane my office in the sky. When you travel like I do, there are certain comforts that become imperative to the travel experience. For me, that is my driver. I had the same driver for over seven years. He would show up fifteen minutes early (which gave me peace of mind). He would come to my door to get my luggage, always with a smile and a treat for my kids (as a mom, this made the goodbye so much easier!). He always ensured I had my passport and asked for my return flight, so he could arrange my pickup. For seven years, his face was familiar, warm, and caring. I knew I could rely on him. I trusted him. Unfortunately, his business started to grow. And like most businesses, there are challenges to scaling up and keeping the customer's experience consistent. I had different drivers; some would get out of the car and some wouldn't. The treats stopped, which meant longer goodbyes and fewer smiles (making it hard for this mamma to get out the door). Sometimes the cars showed up on time, but sometimes not at all. Because of my seven-year loyalty, I kept giving him another chance until recently.

My family and I had landed at the airport, back from a trip to Croatia, and I had arranged to have a car meet us. I'd sent all my details, and guess what? Yep, no car. I took an Uber home with my family that day. And while Uber is inconsistent, I expect inconsistency, which makes it tolerable. I have stopped expecting sugar and receiving salt. I made a change. I stopped using my former driver's car service because my trust had been broken and not repaired. His company had lost not only my weekly pickup and drop-off but also the referrals I would give him. I no longer felt comfortable with putting my name beside his. Disappointment is really just expectations not met. If you set an expectation, you must deliver it or risk losing the trust of your female customer.

Even the longest, most loyal relationships with your customers can go south if you don't meet their expectations and create disappointment. For women, this consistency is even more important. We are often already juggling so many balls that we can't (and won't) put up with a product or brand that doesn't earn the right to our business. Women—for better or worse—seem to multitask at a staggering rate. In an article outlining twenty differences between the male and female brain, it was mentioned that women are more capable of managing multiple tasks, flowing simultaneously, while men get irritated when they have to do several things at the same time. Scientists have found this is due to the gray and white matter within the brain. Women have more white matter, while men rule in the gray-matter category.[11] The gray matter of our brain represents information-processing centers (the ability to take in and process information) and white matter represents the networking of—or connections between—these processing centers (connecting the processing centers). According to a study by the University of California, Irvine, men have approximately six-and-a-half times the amount of gray matter related to general intelligence than women, and women have nearly ten times the amount of white matter related to general intelligence than men.[17] Having the ability to connect information in a multitude of different ways contributes to a women's ability to multitask.

Women often feel the need to take care of everything, which leaves them with a long to-do list and no choice but to get multiple things done at once. When an organization drops the ball or fails to meet her expectations, her juggling act is thrown out of whack, leaving her off-kilter, frustrated, and looking for any other solution.

Write down three companies that you have stopped doing business with and why, and include how each company made you feel.

COMPANY	WHY	HOW DID THEY MAKE YOU FEEL?

I am pretty certain you wrote things down like "I felt angry," "I lost trust," or "I didn't feel important (or I felt like a number) even after years of loyalty." You also may have said you felt disappointed.

Remember, disappointment is simply experiencing unfulfilled hopes and unmet expectations; and it is said to impact decision making in a significant way. Avoid disappointing your female customer and you will keep her purchasing power with your company consistent.

THE KEY TO LONG-TERM RELATIONSHIPS

Maya Angelou said, "People will remember what you said, they will forget what you did, but they will never forget how you made them feel." Emotionally engaged customers are three times more likely to recommend you, three times more likely to purchase from you, less likely to shop around, and much less price sensitive.[13] If you want to be a women-centric business, you should aim for women to fall in love with your brand and emotionally attach themselves to it. When women shop with you, they go on a journey with a critical eye, which is very different than how a man looks at you. A woman will seek to find what she is looking for. She will only give up once she has shared a negative experience with your brand. A man, on the other hand, wants as little friction as possible. He could care less about how it makes him feel. If you provide the service he wants, he will look past the lack of experience you provide. When women interact with you in a positive way, they fall in love with you; the chemicals released in her brain tell her to. While providing a service will satisfy a man, a woman wants and needs an experience as she journeys through your business. She needs to feel all the feels to keep her coming back for more.

Once you recognize that the chemical reactions created when women fall in love are also present when they shop and experience a brand in a positive way, you can understand how powerful the connection is that a woman can feel for your brand. And with this realization comes the obvious solution of tailoring the brand experience to give the female Chief Purchasing Officer exactly what she craves in a strong and meaningful relationship.

Take your female consumer on a journey. Help her fall in love with your people and the brand they represent. Be trustworthy. Focus on how you can make her feel special, rather than the transaction itself. Do this consistently, and the fruits of your labor will bear loyal, referring customers.

FOUR

GETTING TO KNOW HER. GETTING TO KNOW ALL ABOUT HER.

*W*omen want to be treated equally, but that doesn't mean we're the same as men. As we have discovered, women are physiologically different than men. That's simply how women are built, and when you're in the customer-perception business, you need to take that into account. No longer can you live by the golden rule Grandma used to preach: "Treat others the way you want to be treated." It's high time you live by the platinum rule: "Treat others the way *they* need or want to be treated."

In other words, you must find out exactly *how* your female customer wants to be treated. And often, this is not how you would assume it to be. Get to know your Chief Purchasing Officer—what makes her tick. What experience she desires. What a woman wants, not what a business thinks she wants. You can do this by creating a customer persona and by asking your female team members to participate in the information-gathering process. First, let's take a look at a female customer's perception, which is also her reality.

PERCEPTION EQUALS CUSTOM*HER* REALITY

The actuality is that the excellent experience you think you are providing to your female consumer actually isn't first rate—not in her opinion anyway. You may assume you are providing an experience that is welcomed by your female consumers, when in fact, you are instead offering what you feel is right for them. Perception is the reality, and it no longer matters what you think is an exceptional experience. It only matters what the woman feels is an exceptional experience.

The first step to designing an experience for the female consumer is to realize that her perception *is* her reality. When it comes to perception—seeing, feeling, hearing, and sensing things—there is no such thing as objectivity. The consumer sees, hears, and feels from where they stand, not from where you stand.

One Christmas day a few years ago, I had just arrived at my mom's house with the kids for our traditional Christmas festivities: opening a ridiculous amount of presents and stuffing ourselves with turkey. As I was getting out of my car trying to juggle everything (my kids were too excited to help), my grandpa was walking out of the house and came over to help me. He smiled as he approached, reached out his arms, and said, "You know, Katie, I have a few critiques on your most recent podcast . . . you know, on the female consumer." Before I could ask what they were, he continued. "I love what you are talking about. It's everything I spoke about when I was president at the bank. I actually used a formula to help my team put the perception of the customer's experience into perspective." He chuckled. "Us finance guys need to have black-and-white numbers for anything to make sense to us. Anyway . . . the formula I used to coach my team was 'Happiness equals your perspective in line with the customer's expectations.'"

I put my armload of gifts down on the hood of the car and turned to face him.

"Tell me more," I said.

"Well, all employees feel they are giving a great experience from their perspective but often they don't actually meet the customer's expectations, which leads to disappointment. So in order for the customer to be happy, employees need to ensure their perspective is in line with the customer's expectations."

Almost in unison we said, "And then deliver on those expectations!" We broke into laughter.

"Grandpa, do I have permission to add this to my book?"

"I would be honored," he said. "But one more thing, Katie. This equation should zero out. The perception of the experience you deliver must come in line with the expectations of the customer. If not, your business won't deliver."

The reason I share this story with you is because aiming for customer happiness is not a new idea or a revolution. Unfortunately, since my grandfather left the bank over forty years ago, businesses have rarely met customer expectations, and employees don't adjust their perspectives to come in line with their customers. Even more rare is looking at expectations by gender to understand how to tailor the experience for women. When are we going to wake up and aim to make our customers happy, regardless of what we think the experience should be? In order to achieve custom*her* reality we must aim to make the female consumer happy. We must level our perspective so it meets her expectations. In the previous chapter I mentioned that disappointment and broken hearts are simply expectations failed to be delivered on, and this little formula demonstrates that beautifully.

HAPPINESS = YOUR PERSPECTIVE IN LINE WITH CUSTOMER EXPECTATIONS

I am now going to show you how this "Happiness" formula is put into action with a real-life case study. In the course of my career, I have had the honor and privilege to consult with one of the fastest-growing hospitality organizations in the world. Celebrity Cruises is the epitome of being female-focused from the inside out. Not only is their president and CEO a woman, 30 percent of the staff aboard their ships are female, and they walk the talk when it comes to giving back and fighting equality on all fronts. With a woman at the helm, the experiences on board their ships are very intentionally designed to incorporate all guests; however, you can definitely tell there has been special attention paid to the needs of the female guests.

I was recently on a ship doing leadership training with the executive leadership team. I've become known on board as the "chief inspirational officer," so while I am in guest areas, I wear a name tag with that title (it's a perfect example of creating an experience for me!). Wearing this name tag has also given me the ability to interact with guests on a whole new level. One evening after the late show I was stopped by a female guest who unfortunately had had a frustrating experience on board. She was traveling with her family: her husband, three kids, and her parents. One of her boys had just returned from his first year at college and (to her surprise) was very excited to spend time with Mom. In preparation for this trip, she had requested a table for eight in the main dining room so they could enjoy dinners together as a family. They arrived at the main dining room on the first night and were told that the ship could only accommodate six and not eight for dinner. As she told me the story, she had tears in her eyes because all she had wanted to do was connect with her family and create a few memories (especially with her son who'd returned from college). I told her I was really happy she'd approached me and told me how she was feeling, assuring her we would take care of her and her family . . . and we did. Every night from then on, the whole family sat together at dinner.

Let's stop there for a minute and look at this based on my grandfather's formula:

Happiness for the guest would mean that she could eat with her entire family.

The crew perspective was that they'd done what they could to accommodate her within their restraints of seating in the restaurant.

The guest's expectation was that she had made the arrangements prior to boarding and the crew would accommodate her request.

Breaking this example down shows you that the guest's expectation wasn't met, which meant that she (and her family) was not happy. And as a mother—and a female guest—this "unhappiness" is intensified because women feel emotions more deeply than men do (we can blame our limbic brain for that!), which makes understanding the female customer's expectations extremely important.

Celebrity is a world-class operation, and once they understood her expectations and feelings, they did everything they could to make it right.

What I love about Celebrity is they focus not on the mechanics of making an experience right but on how the experience will make the guest feel special, and that goes a long way with the decision maker. The story doesn't end there. In true Celebrity fashion, the team made sure the entire family had an opportunity to dine in an exclusive restaurant on board, turning a dining experience into a memory that Mom would never forget.

I saw her a few days later at the yoga studio, and she thanked me for listening to her, hearing how the situation made her feel, and turning the experience right-side up. Her expectations had been met and in return she was happy with the experience she had received. She shared with me that she will now only sail with Celebrity moving forward because she feels taken care of. As long as you are willing to look past what needs to be done and start focusing on how it will make someone *feel*, meeting their expectations, you will create happiness. This is exactly what the Chief Purchasing Officer looks for when making vacation decisions: How will my family feel, what memories will we create, and will we connect as a family during this time?

CLOSING THE DELIVERY GAP

When I train organizations or speak at conferences about the female consumer, I always emphasize the enormous gap that exists between the *perception* of the experience provided by retailers and the *reality* of what customers feel they're receiving. Have you ever been reading a negative review on a customer satisfaction survey and found yourself puzzled? You run through the scenario and ask yourself how this customer could have complained. You did everything right—or so you thought. This is the delivery gap: your perception of the experience provided versus the customer's reality.

Check out this sobering statistic: Ninety-one percent of women feel misunderstood by advertisers.[1] In a study of 362 businesses, management-consulting company Bain found that 80 percent believe their business offers a superior proposition or experience. However, only 8 percent of customers hold that same view. The extent of this difference is extraordinary. Bain calls this disparity the "delivery gap."[2]

This delivery gap grows in size when organizations are not in tune with their customers and are not paying attention to how their *customers* want to be sold to or approached. When you're serving a woman, it's even more important to pay close attention to the experience gap.

In all industries, regardless of the service or product, one thing never changes: Organizations are serving and selling to humans. And on the receiving end, women are at the helm. Closing the experience gap is critical to captivating and keeping your customer's attention, especially when it comes to women. Everyone has the ability to compare the price and quality of virtually any product or service; but once the consumer is done doing their research, the only thing left to do is create an emotional connection, making the experience the differentiator. This is an important fact to note for all consumers; however, it is vital to winning over the vote of the female Chief Purchasing Officer.

Remember, physiologically, the limbic system of a woman is larger and deeper than the limbic system of a man. This makes the emotional connection—the overall experience—that she may be seeking even more prevalent. Some sort of trust must be established between an organization and the consumer, or your consumer will not likely be compelled to say yes to a brand.

The good news is that companies can close this huge gap by taking the necessary steps to understand a female consumer's needs, wants, and desires so she feels recognized and validated. By designing your consumer brand experience from a female's point of view, you will be able to close the gap between perception and reality.

Before I move on, I feel compelled to share how all this information can help not only at work but in your personal life, too. The number one way to motivate anyone is to find out what they want and use that information to move them into action. This is as true in business as it is at home, and now you know why women are the way they are. You know what makes men and women different. You have some new information that can help motivate all the women in your life.

I was speaking at the New Car Dealer Association of Utah for the second time in late 2019 on the topic of the female consumer. We spent an entire day getting to know her, understanding her wants, needs, and desires, and of course developing ways to tailor the experience these dealers provide to the decision maker in their dealerships. At the end of the day, everyone was excited to be armed with this new knowledge, ready to establish a true custom*her* experience and meet her expectations. Well, it wasn't until a few days after the session that my Chief Strategy Officer received a phone call from one of the dealers who'd attended. She immediately picked up the phone and called me right after the conversation. "Katie, Tim called me. He absolutely loved your session and wants you to come work with his team." Of course, I thought that was fantastic! She continued, "But what's even cooler is he shared a story with me about how this affected him personally. Katie, he thanked us for opening his eyes. He and his wife were having a disagreement and instead of his normal, reactive response, he remembered what you taught him. He took a deep breath, listened, tried to uncover her expectations, and then delivered on them. Tim mentioned that because of your training he was able to see things from her point of view [her perceptions] and put himself in her shoes. His wife thanked him and was smiling after the disagreement! Katie, I think that your message is not just for businesses, but for humans." I hung up the phone with a grin that stretched from ear to ear. The words on these pages, although written for businesses, can also be used to improve the relationships with all the women in your life.

Taking the time to understand your female customer and giving her what she wants and needs will go a long way in tailoring the experience you offer. One way to do this effectively is by involving the female members of your company team as you research your female consumer.

GET YOUR TEAM INVOLVED (ESPECIALLY THE LADIES)

Ask your female employees what experiences they look for and use that to start journeying through your female consumer's eyes, designing an experience with which she can fall in love.

A great exercise to perform with your team members is to do a walk-through from the female decision maker's point of view. Encourage and empower your female team members to speak up and have a voice! The improved atmosphere will also make a considerable impact on the work experience for your female employees.

Walk your team through the entire consumer experience and ask them the following questions:

- What do you see that could be changed to improve the atmosphere specifically? What would make it more female-friendly?

- What would your mother, sister, wife, or daughter like to experience when they do business with our company?

- In your experience, what do other retailers (outside of our industry) provide to enhance their atmosphere, making it more female-friendly?

By involving the female members of your team from the very beginning, you will be intentional where most companies are not; this perspective will help you design an experience that will earn female consumers' trust, loyalty, and referrals. You must be willing to look beyond your current knowledge and strategically focus on the functions and opportunities that your competitors fail to see. And how else can you do that? Simple. Begin with establishing a consumer persona.

THE "CONSUMER PERSONA"

Customer segmentation is very important in any marketing effort but it is equally (if not more) important when designing a brand experience. Not only does it help you to create and communicate a targeted marketing approach, but it also arms your frontline team with a basic road map of the customers they interact with on a daily basis. In addition, it prompts your team's emotional connection with the customer, helping them to go into every interaction with compassion and empathy.

When you start by understanding the emotions of your customers, you will have a better chance at rallying your team around the needs and wants of your customers. Identifying what your female consumers think, feel, say, and do will help you to understand them, which is a vital piece to creating and feeling compassion toward your customers.

The female consumer's decision-making process is driven by how she feels, not by the item in question she wants to purchase. Understanding *Her* and creating a custom*Her* experience must be emotionally driven and human focused. She needs to be understood. This means that your typical methods of customer segmentation aren't going to get you very far with the female consumer. Categories such as age, sex, marital status, and location (urban, suburban, rural) won't reveal the details about the female consumer that will help you design an experience that says, "I understand you."

A consumer persona flushes out details on each of your customers. I will describe how to develop a consumer persona in this chapter. But remember: don't assume anything—keep your eye on the prize. Women are the most influential consumers.

There are many ways to get the information you need to create a consumer persona: face-to-face or telephone interviews, surveys, Google research, and focus groups, to name a few. One of the most impactful strategies (regardless of the method) is to involve your team. By doing this, you are allowing them to discover with you and be part of the process, and you will (without even trying) create more "aha" moments, trust, and better execution. Your team will inevitably be on your side and will gladly execute what you ask of them. They will also have a greater understanding of the Chief Purchasing Officer. It's important to remember when creating a consumer persona for the female consumer that she wants to be understood first as a woman and second as a consumer. Having this knowledge will allow your team to put themselves in her shoes, which will lead to more compassion and empathy for the woman standing in front of them.

LIFE STAGES

When creating a female consumer persona, you will want to break out your female consumers into life stages. There has been a change in the female's life journey, so typical segmentation becomes outdated. You can't assume anything, because everything is possible in a woman's life today.

Identifying life stages, however, will allow you to identify what influences your female consumer and how she influences others; what her challenges or fears are; how you can help overcome these; and how she wants to be treated while interacting with you in a much more meaningful way.

Consider these life stages when creating the female consumer persona:

SINGLE—A woman who does not have a partner and is self-reliant. She usually lives on her own or with a roommate. A young, single female is often in search of the answer to the question, "Who am I?" or "How do I want to be known/defined?" A more mature single woman (who maybe has been divorced, but always has life experience) knows who she is and what she wants.

MARRIED—She has just gone from me to we. She lives with her partner and is now making decisions not only for herself, but also for the couple and the home. Her thinking is much broader and the importance of the fiscal impact of her purchases on the "unit" is of greater importance. She may still carry some student debt or have purchased her first home. She will focus a little less on "I" and a little more on "we" (although she still makes significant time for herself).

YOUNG FAMILY—A decision has been made and now there are three (or four or five) in the family. In my case, I went from "we" to four with the arrival of our twins! As a first-time (or second- or third-time) mom, decisions become harder to make. A woman's focus naturally becomes all about the kids. She is starving for the "me" time that once existed, and when she needs to go shopping, she prays that her kids behave or that there is a play area to drop them in (*big* win for IKEA!). Finances are usually tighter because kids have sports, clothes, and all the things that make kids so expensive to raise. The female with a young family also may have decided to stay home with the kids (or maybe Dad has), which also can impact finances.

This life stage is a big shift in a female consumer's decision-making process, and it will remain that way for the next fifteen to eighteen years (possibly longer).

EMPTY NESTER—The kids have moved out! This more mature female and her partner are at a stage in life when they are getting to know themselves and each other all over again. The female is finally traveling more, taking more time for herself, and her decisions become less about the kids (maybe a little about the grandkids, but hey, Grandma can send them home at the end of the day!) and more about her needs. She may splurge and buy the car or designer purse she always wanted. Either way, life has slowed down and she is enjoying every moment of her newfound (kid-less) freedom. At this stage of life, she is still heading to work every day (or maybe back to work after raising her kids).

PLATINUM YEARS—Do I hear retirement bells? Hobbies, lawn care, lunches with friends, and time with grandkids become her focus. The female consumer at this stage is hosting family dinners and finds joy in the slow pace of life. There is usually more travel (bucket-list travel!) and less worry about financial burdens. She loves to connect and have relationships. She can start to feel lonely (especially if she has lost a partner), and the time outside the home may mean a lot to her.

WHAT DOES IT ALL MEAN?

Once you establish your customer's life stage, you'll want to use that information to home in on the answers to three key questions:

1. What are her needs?
2. What does she fear?
3. What are her goals?

Here are a few questions that will help you uncover her needs, fears, and goals, while thinking about your female customers as women first and customers second:

- What are her favorite brands?
- What are her favorite websites or sources for news?
- Which social media channels does she use?
  - › Twitter? _____
  - › Facebook? _____
  - › LinkedIn? _____
  - › Instagram? _____
  - › Other? _____
- What are her personal goals?
- What are her professional goals?

- What are her family goals?

- What matters most to her?

- What is her biggest desire?

- What is her greatest fear?

- If she could change one thing about her life stage, what would it be?

- What are three problems she may be experiencing during each life stage?

  › What does she need in order to solve these problems?

  › What is the worst thing that can happen to her if her problems are not eventually resolved?

  › How do these three problems make her a customer of your business?

- What is it that she really wants more than anything else?

- What would she be willing to pay almost anything for?

Use this information to create your female consumer personas. Create a one-page document per life stage. Your consumer personas should not only be used to design brand standards for her journey through your business, but also as a part of the brand experience training you provide to each team member and should be added to your Brand Experience Playbook. Every team member should know who your female customers are, what her goals are, and what they need most and fear. This will arm your team with the ability to provide a genuine and compassionate experience for the Chief Purchasing Officer. Once you've gotten to know who your female consumer is, you can begin to prepare for the type of experience she wants.

FIVE

TAKING A JOURNEY
THROUGH HER EYES

*N*ow that you have a foundational understanding of your female consumer as a woman first and a customer second, it's time to put that information to the test. Put yourself in her shoes! This is much easier to do, of course, if you've done your research and have also included your female team members in the process.

When developing a customer experience program, you always want to see through the lens of the customer. As I've stated, it's vital to remember that perception is reality; an experience that is good for you may not meet the expectations of your customers (especially the female customer). The next step is mapping out your female customer experience journey.

MAPPING OUT THE JOURNEY

Customer journey mapping is a way to deconstruct a customer's experience with a product or service as a series of steps and themes. Dissecting your customer's journey encourages your team to think about the customer's needs effectively, identifying pain points and opportunities at each touchpoint in their journey when doing business with you.

A customer touchpoint is any medium along a customer's brand journey that engages with them. It is the "step through time" that your customers experience. The key is to keep the focus on the customer, not you. Journey mapping is a crucial exercise to close the delivery gap, bringing you and your team closer to understanding through *her* eyes, not yours. The customer check-in process at a hotel would be an example of a touchpoint—a step a customer needs to take before they enjoy their time at the hotel. Do you have your female customer's journey mapped? If so, ask yourself, does my team have an understanding of how each person/department/touchpoint affects the other? If the answer is yes, bravo! If you answered no, then you have some work to do (either to create the journey map or to give your team a greater understanding of the overall end-to-end experience).

I am going to take a guess that no matter which camp you're in (with a journey map or not), you might not have taken the time to see things from the female point of view. This doesn't mean you need to have two separate journey maps; what this does mean is that you need to have specific brand standards at each touchpoint tailored for the female decision maker.

I'm—ironically—going to use a very "male" event to describe the intricate and important process of journey mapping. I'm talking about Formula One, the *big* race! Building a Formula One (F1) car is an intricate process: Engineering, materials science, and cutting-edge software come together as these machines are developed and designed from scratch each year. The McLaren F1 team might change up to 70 percent of a car's mechanical structure per racing season. The car is continually monitored with more than two hundred built-in sensors, generating 25 billion data points on a Grand Prix weekend.

Communication and collaboration of the 1,000-plus-member teams is integral to success as the team continually measures, analyzes, and evaluates every detail with a maniacal focus on how the slightest modification of any part affects all other aspects and the overall performance. Based on these sensor results, the team is able to map the journey of the car, and can rebuild and fine-tune these cars for each race.

Does that sound familiar?

Within your organization, there are also myriad customer touchpoints that act like the car sensors, which produce an abundance of data points for each interaction, telling you and your team how you are impacting the customer journey. If you pay attention to how your customers "vote with their feet," you will know at which touchpoint your team "drops the ball," leaving your customers dissatisfied.

Having your customer's journey mapped allows you to pinpoint where you are succeeding or failing to satisfy your customers. I caution you, however, to focus not only on specific touchpoints, but on how each of those touchpoints works with the others. If you only focus on a specific touchpoint, your team misses the big picture, and the customer will suffer somewhere along the way. Each touchpoint along the journey is connected and impacts one another. Just like the F1 team, one small change affects the performance of the vehicle; each touchpoint affects the entire journey your customer has with your brand.

While it is essential to pay attention to the details (or the one touchpoint that doesn't seem to be working), you also have to look at how those touchpoints work together and contribute to the overall customer journey. Service is manifested everywhere your organization touches the customer; therefore, you must intentionally manage the service experience beyond the obvious customer touchpoints.

A preview of Forrester's annual production report warned that in 2018, thirty percent of companies "will see further declines in CX performance, and those declines will translate into a net loss of a point of growth."[1] Why? Customer Experience (CX) initiatives tackled only the touchpoints that weren't performing to put an early score on the board.

You will lose every time by only focusing on the "low-hanging fruit" or the touchpoint that is not performing; this is a Band-Aid solution. Business owners must make CX an integral part of their overall brand experience strategy and identify how each touchpoint impacts each other and the brand experience, inclusively.

Step out in front of the competition by looking at your business's overall journey from 30,000 feet. Bridge the performance gaps between touchpoints. And just as the 1,000-member team focuses on how to improve the performance of an F1 car each year, your team needs the same focus to enhance the experience you provide to your customers.

STEPS TO BEGIN THE JOURNEY

If you want your brand experience performance to be top-notch for your female customers, you will have to work hard to ensure a seamless experience throughout their entire journey. Here are four things your business can do to start the change and improve your overall brand experience.

1. *Review (or create) a journey map.*
   Bridge the gap between individually focused touchpoints and a holistic brand journey. A journey map is a way to deconstruct

a customer's experience, collecting all the customer's steps through time with a 30,000-foot vantage point. When you string all the steps through time together, you and your team can start to see the forest through the trees and realize how many moving parts go into an experience with your brand. This is very important because every team member's interaction with the female consumer affects the next touchpoint she interacts with. To have a comprehensive view of the customer's experience means that your team can comprehend all the different moving parts of the customer's journey and how they are all intimately interconnected and explicable only by reference to the whole. Your team must be able to understand the whole journey in order to execute their portion of the journey. They each play a part in every moment the customer experiences when doing business with them; understanding this amplifies the importance their role holds.

To create a journey map, I suggest you bring together a team of leaders and frontline team members. You will want to identify all the possible ways your brand interacts with its customers. Every business is different, and your touchpoints will vary. I have listed a few journey maps using touchpoints for three industries:

HOTEL
    Online/Social
    Room reservation (phone call or online)
    Phone call or email confirmation
    Arrival
    Check-in
    Service recovery
    Checkout

RESTAURANT

> Online/Social
>
> Reservation (phone or online)
>
> Arrival
>
> Wait time (if applicable)
>
> Seating
>
> Meal
>
> Check
>
> Lasting impression

SPA

> Online/Social
>
> Reservation (phone or online)
>
> Arrival
>
> Wait time
>
> Treatment
>
> Payment/Lasting impression

It is the accumulation of small moments over time that amounts to an experience worth coming back for in the mind of the female consumer. The act of defining those small touchpoints and showing your team how these points work together is the first step in the right direction.

2. *Ask your team, "How do we make an experience for her at each touchpoint?"*

As a team, while keeping your female consumers in mind, go through each touchpoint and brainstorm how you can turn her journey into an interaction she enjoys. You will need to look past the operational expectations and focus on what makes your customers feel special. If you focus on ways to make your customer feel this way, you will naturally complete the expected standards while connecting with her on an emotional level. Remember: you must see the person, not just the dollar she brings you. Other questions your team can answer while brainstorming are—

› What are female consumers saying about our company now?

› What do we want them to say about our company in the future? (Use your future idealism to craft an experience that will deliver on her expectations.)

Also ask your female team members to share stories about their best brand experience and what the company specifically did to create an impact. Consider taking your team on a pragmatic journey as well! Have them go and experience different brands and return with the ways these brands made an impact on them or what they observed in regard to a female consumer. No matter which way you decide to get the brainstorm flowing, this exercise is vital to making the shift from a transactional service to an interactional experience for your female consumers.

Once you have compiled these ideas by touchpoint, dwindle the list to the top five ways your business can create an experience throughout the female journey. Add this to your current brand experience standards or use it as the start of your brand standards.

3. *Anticipate her needs.*

Use the first two steps as a launchpad to creating an experience she can't live without. Don't stop there. Continue to urge your team to identify ways to create these experiences. Empower your team to be aware of her needs and listen for cues that she gives your business throughout the journey to provide an anticipatory experience that tells the female consumer that your business is listening to her. Unfortunately, there is no system or process that can help your team members do this one. This is truly dependent on how your team flips the lens and listens to (and hears) the customer, while being aware of how they can provide experiences that are both unexpected and exciting. You can definitely practice getting better at this as a team. Give the team scenarios or stories and ask them what they heard on their brand experiential journeys, and how they can anticipate the customer's needs.

I was recently on the receiving end of a brand experience that made a huge impact on me. I had traveled to Singapore to work with the leaders aboard one of their company's cruise ships. It took me twenty-nine hours before I even reached the ship. As you can imagine, I was exhausted. When I got to my suite, I had never been so excited to see a bed! I quickly got into my comfy clothes and slid under the covers. Just as I was about to close my eyes, the phone rang. I answered with a groggy "Hello?" A sweet voice on the other end said, "Good afternoon, Mrs. Mares, this is the documentation officer. We require your passport before we sail." I let out a big huff and said, "Can I bring it down to you later? I have a pounding headache and I was just lying down to take a nap." There was a slight pause and the documentation officer continued. "Unfortunately not, Mrs. Mares. I can, however, come get it from you." I thanked her and about five minutes later there was a knock on my door. I got out of bed and opened the door to hand her my passport. To my surprise, she had a bottle of water and aspirin in her hand! She smiled at me and said, "I hope this helps you feel better, Mrs. Mares.

Thank you for staying up to provide me with your passport. If you need anything else, please let me know." I closed the door with a smile on my face.

It gets better! The next morning my butler greeted me by name and asked if my headache was gone. He then escorted me to the medical center in case I needed any more aspirin throughout the day. When I returned to my room there was aspirin and water waiting for me.

I tell this story often because it is such an amazing example of how you can anticipate a customer's needs with very little information. All I told the documentation officer was that I had a headache and two people took it upon themselves to show they cared by listening, showing compassion, and anticipating that I might need an aspirin to take away my headache, and a bottle of water to swallow it. My female limbic brain told me—much more strongly than a man's—that I felt cared for and had experienced empathy from the employees. This is a feeling I will remember.

These moments in a woman's experiences will only heighten her emotional attachment to your brand; remember, a woman's limbic system is almost double that of a man's, making these moments very significant to her and how she feels about you and your brand.

There are many ways your team members can anticipate your female consumer's needs; you have to pay attention to what they tell you!

4. *Pay Attention to the Atmosphere You Create.*

Atmosphere and ambience impact the overall feeling the customer has when they are doing business with you. The tone or mood of the four walls you host your customers in affects the mood of your customers, and women, more than men, care about how they feel in your space.

In what seems like a lifetime ago, I dedicated the first part of my career to developing a customer's experience, including the atmosphere and ambience in which they shopped, through store design, product displays, and customer experiences within retail locations. I was the head of merchandising for a Canadian shoe company. I had the *best* job. It was my responsibility to make the hundreds of shoes at our locations silently sell themselves through their placement, the store's music, seating, furniture layout, lighting, and even smell. Each week I would analyze the sell-through rate based off the reactions of the customers through the number of units sold from the displays and overall store ambience. I would make the changes necessary based on my analysis.

It's important to note that our shoe stores were merchandised to suit the female customer. Eighty percent of the stores' assortment was for women, while only 20 percent was for male shoppers; the store setup reflected our desire to appeal to the majority consumer: the woman. We softened the lighting, which is always more flattering, changed the placement and height of mirrors, the music, the placement of merchandise by style and heel height, and increased the comfortability of the chairs in the store, all of which enticed the female consumer. We even created little nooks for moms shopping with kids. During my time in this position, I would travel across Canada visiting and analyzing stores and the reactions of the female consumer. I learned a thing or two about what she wants in an atmosphere *and* what she responds to overall during a brand experience. And it's *completely* different than what a man desires.

SIX

WHAT THE CHIEF PURCHASING OFFICER WANTS

*N*ow that (hopefully) you've researched your female consumer and understand what makes her tick, gotten input from the females in your life, and mapped out the journey with touchpoints, it's time to put it all into play.

Obviously, tailoring your brand experience to women means just that: tailoring it to *your* distinctive female consumer. However, there are some universal truths about branding to women, which are extremely important and can give you a jumping-off point if you're struggling to create a memorable interactional experience for your female customer instead of a simple transactional one.

CREATE A HEDONIC EXPERIENCE

Through some research, I found out that women will pay 32 percent more in a hedonic atmosphere as opposed to a utilitarian atmosphere.[1] A *what* as opposed to a *what?* Let me explain. A hedonic atmosphere is one that heightens your sensations and speaks directly to the limbic brain (how a person feels and the memory of the experience). And of course, you remember that a woman's limbic brain is much larger and deeper than a man's, meaning that feelings and memories are more important to the female consumer. For a woman (and some men), shopping is an experience that satisfies an emotional purpose, and as I stated earlier in this book, often the chase (or shopping journey) that the customer goes on causes arousal and enjoyment. Men are on a mission and women are on a journey. Those customers that enjoy the thrill of the journey love it not because of the purchase itself, but due to the atmosphere in which they shop. This puts a big emphasis on the atmosphere you create.

On the other hand, a utilitarian atmosphere, which men prefer, is related to creating an experience that makes it easy to fulfill a task.[2] To create a utilitarian atmosphere, you should focus on atmospherics such as architecture, cleanliness, floor space allocation, flooring, and color scheme of the store. The primary focus is to make it easy to find the product and get the customer in and out in a timely fashion— with the task they set out to complete, completed.

In my many years of experience designing stores, floor plans, lighting placement, music selection, et cetera, it has always proven successful to build your atmosphere to satisfy the customers that prefer a hedonic experience with attention to ease of shopping for those who need to "get in and get out."

Creating a hedonic, female-friendly atmosphere may seem like an obvious solution to making your female customer base feel comfortable when interacting with your business. However, in my experience, it's usually the most overlooked opportunity. If you want hedonic customers to revisit your location, you should focus on the style of the store, floor space allocation, product presentation, sound level, lighting, and the interior material. These aspects lend themselves to an overall, balanced ambience that heightens the senses and adds fun into the mix for a memorable experience she wants to enjoy again and again.

At the turn of the twentieth century, the places women went to shop were dark and gloomy, and no one wanted to spend time there. However, in the 1920s, merchants started to see the light and created spaces that were welcoming and warm, turning these shops into places anyone would dream of visiting.

When well-lit and glamorous department stores like Macy's, Marshall Fields, Wanamaker's, and Altman's first opened in major cities like New York, Chicago, and San Francisco, middle-class women flocked to these emporiums to enjoy their soothing and idyllic interiors. Advertisers encouraged women to come to the stores, not to purchase, but for pleasure, conversation, and to get lost in the atmosphere the business had created. For the first time, stores and brands focused on the hedonic atmospheres that females craved. Women did not spend countless hours in these stores simply to "buy things" (although they did), but to enjoy the pleasure the spaces brought them.

The hedonic atmosphere is not just for the brick-and-mortar locations. Women do a lot of shopping online while their kids sleep (and in my case, while I'm in my office in the sky). Now being dubbed the "webmosphere," the atmosphere of a female's online shopping experience can also fulfill the need for a hedonic experience. Results from a study show that if web marketers design web stores with freedom of movement during navigation and adequate music for their customers, they could be able to generate more positive responses from econsumers (satisfaction and approach responses), and in turn, improve their online sales. The study revealed that the conscious designing of web environments creates positive effects in users and increases favorable consumer responses (for example, site revisiting, browsing, etc.).[3] When marketers design web interfaces in order to entice consumers, they are utilizing web atmospherics.

Whether you have a location to visit or are an online retailer (or both), you need to ensure your atmosphere is conducive to the needs of the world's most influential consumer. Your female customers consciously decide what they need, research it, want to visit your business to touch and feel it, but what they may not realize is that the atmosphere in which they do this makes a big impact on their decision-making process. How the customer feels when she is shopping will sway her one way or the other. Your team's appearance, the entrance to your location, the cleanliness, the way you answer the phone, and the freedom of movement on your website all speak to the customer.

Ask yourself (and answer honestly), "Is the atmosphere of my business female-friendly? Does it reflect a hedonic state?" The key is to make her feel at home, creating an atmosphere that is comfortable, warm, and inviting.

HEDONIC HOW-TO

There are many ways to create a female-friendly environment; the trick is to look at the atmosphere through her eyes and flip the lens. Tailoring the atmosphere for the female consumer will result in her feeling comfortable, which will contribute to her trust in your brand. And surprise: our brains have something to do with it! According to an article in *Scientific American*, women have a larger corpus callosum, which is the connection of nerve tissue between the left and right sides of the brain. Women use this bigger corpus callosum to employ both hemispheres of their brains to navigate problems more rapidly than men, who are using predominantly the left side of their brains.[4] Women have the ability to communicate and process information with both sides of their brain, where men primarily use their left hemisphere, which is in charge of logically processing facts. How does that pertain to shopping and the impact the atmosphere you provide has on the female consumer? Because of the difference in brain structure, men look for and are attracted to a more "mission- or task-oriented" experience, whereas women are more "discovery-oriented" shoppers who will pivot their goals based on how they feel during their experience with your business.

There is a little bar called Prohibition in Salt Lake City, Utah. I absolutely love this place. When you enter the storefront, a woman dressed in a 1920s-style flapper dress asks, "What ails ya?" You then tell her what pain you have, and she prescribes you a drink. Then another woman opens a hidden door concealed in a wall and reveals the bar. You walk through the opening and it's as if you've taken a time machine back to the 1920s. Red velvet fabric adorns the walls; there's smoky lighting and antique fixtures. It is sexy, provocative, and fun!

On my last visit, I talked to one of the managers. I was curious about how, in a very conservative state such as Utah, this type of venue would capture both the male and female customer. Her eyes lit up as she explained how they were able to achieve an atmosphere that speaks to both sexes. She leaned in closer as if she was about to tell me a big secret. "You see, the men like to know what they are going to get out of the experience right from the get-go, and our name 'Prohibition' does that. They know they can come in, get a drink, and enjoy a 'prohibited' experience. Male customers instantly picture pretty girls serving drinks behind closed doors. Women, on the other hand, appreciate the details that create the atmosphere, for example, how the 'pretty girls' are dressed in accurate period costumes, the dim lighting, velvet curtains, and the mystery of how they enter through the camouflaged wall." She glanced around the room and back at me. "If you look around, you can see how the women don't feel intimidated and the men are enjoying themselves. It's because we've curated the atmosphere to reflect the needs of both men and women."

I took a look around. She was right, and what she'd described was a blend of utilitarian (functional) atmosphere—designed to be useful or practical—so that men get what they want, and a hedonic atmosphere—relating to or characterized by pleasure—for the females. The women come because they love the feelings the atmosphere provokes.

The atmosphere you create can reflect both a utilitarian and hedonic state. Often you must build the basic utilitarian and functional atmosphere as the foundation before you sprinkle the fairy dust to create magic, elevating the experience to emphasize the senses that speak to the Chief Purchasing Officer. The goal is to elevate her senses to create a shopping experience for her that will resonate, because the basic utilitarian atmosphere that most brands create will never live up to her expectations. Focus on the experiential value of the shopping experience so it includes fun and aesthetic pleasure for the imagination while elevating sensory pleasure. Below is a list of questions that can help you transform a utilitarian atmosphere into one that stimulates the senses.

Here are some things to look for:

- How does the energy feel?

- Is the music appropriate?

- How vast is your magazine selection?

- Do you have a seating area? If so, is it comfortable?

- Do you have fresh flowers?

- Is the scent of the atmosphere appealing?

- What is the temperature? Is it too cold, and if it is, do you have blankets or heaters available?

- Is your lighting fluorescent or warm and soft? Women want to feel relaxed and comfortable; fluorescent lighting does not promote this feeling.

- Are the colors warm and inviting?

- If you have washrooms, are they bright, clean, and stocked with female amenities?

- Does your product placement reflect what she is looking for?

Whether I am keynoting or doing a full training on the female consumer, I almost always ask the male business leaders in the room to visit the women's washroom and report back to me what they see, now that they know what a woman is truly seeking. Their responses are priceless. The men in the audience have almost never been in the women's washroom and are often shocked at how stark it is. The washroom is the always the first thing they change when they get back to their offices or stores. They add comfortable seating areas, female amenities such as high-end hand soap and lotion, tampons, pads, softer lighting, and replace harsh, brown paper towels with softer, thicker white options. Without fail, I hear from one of their team members about the difference it has made and how many female customers and employees have positively commented on the changes.

We are all busy, leading a crazy life of to-do lists with a "get s**t done" mentality. It's certainly easy to overlook the most obvious need for change. I challenge you to step off your hamster wheel and journey through her eyes. You will be blown away by all the little things you can change that will make a huge impact on your business's atmosphere and her experience.

The goal is to "see" the atmosphere through *her* eyes and consider what she may feel when she journeys through your business. Closing the delivery gap between your perspective and hers can only be done by flipping the lens, taking the time to understand what she wants in an atmosphere, and making the necessary changes to create an atmosphere in which she wants to spend time.

DELIVER A REAL RELATIONSHIP

Relationships are very real and important to the female consumer. Remember what I wrote about oxytocin, the bonding hormone, and how it affects women more than men? It feels good for the female consumer to create relationships that lead to trust, connection, and loyalty. That's why women value relationships so strongly and why companies must work to create these relationships in order to gain trust and brand loyalty. One of the biggest differences between men and women is this: Women want to build a relationship with your brand, but a man is happy to just complete the purchase. Women's limbic brains are almost double the size of a man's; physiologically, we crave connection.

A quote from the famous book *Men Are from Mars and Women Are from Venus* by John Gray depicts this well: "Men are motivated when they feel needed, while women are motivated when they feel cherished."[5] For men to "feel needed," the product needs to solve a problem that helps him live without stress; the product you are selling must fulfill a purpose in his life. Women, on the other hand, want to feel comfortable, valued, and cherished by the company she chooses to business with. The dictionary states that *cherish* is "to protect and care for (someone) lovingly." Have you ever cherished someone that you didn't have a relationship with? The quick answer is no. In order to cherish someone, you must care for them, and caring comes from the emotional connection you have with that person—the relationship. Knowing that women crave connection and want to feel cherished makes creating a relationship with your female consumer on the top of the priority list.

As a leader, you must shift your mindset in order to stop thinking of your female consumer as someone you are "getting" value from and view her as someone to whom you are "giving" value. When you make this shift, you start to focus on the woman you are serving. Read that again: the woman *you are serving.*

I was standing in a boardroom speaking with a group of business leaders—the third group I had worked with that week—training them on how to help their team deliver a genuine experience in order to build real relationships. As I was giving examples of the importance of being genuine with their customers (especially the female customers), I could see everyone's eyes start to dart side to side, and in one case even roll. One of the leaders decided to pipe up and ask, "How do you expect us to be genuine when we don't know the person?" What these leaders didn't know was that all three groups I'd addressed that week had revealed the same concern, which initially shocked me.

In my usual fashion, I asked for permission to be honest with the group, and they agreed. "We have a bigger concern if you can't be genuine with your customers and build relationships with them." Now their eyes widened. I continued. "Who keeps a roof over your head and food on your table? This company, right?" They all nodded. "Well, what does this company need in order to do that? Customers, right?" They nodded again while I looked into all of their eyes. "If that is not enough reason to show your customers genuine care and want to create a relationship with them, then you have the wrong people on your team." I didn't stop there. "How many women do you serve daily? More than 50 percent of your customer base, right?" They all nodded in unison and the tension in the room started to dissipate as they realized how important the relationships they created with their biggest customer base were to the success of the company, and therefore, the success of their families.

I have had this conversation with many organizations all over the world. Being genuine, creating real relationships, and cherishing your customers will not only benefit the customer and the company, but also the person serving the customer. Yet companies I work with still give me the excuse of not having enough time to create deep and meaningful relationships with their customers.

Does that sound familiar? Thinking that building relationships and being genuine are a waste of time is a big mistake. Ultimately, you are telling your customers, especially the females, that they are not a priority to you or your business. Creating an emotional connection with your female consumer should be your number one priority. Pay attention to them, showing compassion and empathy. Be genuine, and don't forget that being human is okay; it's preferred, and revealing vulnerabilities says, "I am human too." It's no different than when a woman says to her partner, "I'm not feeling emotionally connected, and I need that connection to feel safe and intimate with you." When you create a relationship with your female consumer, you build up an emotional connection that allows her to trust and feel comfortable with your business.

It is that connection and relationship that leads to trust. Trust leads to purchases and loyalty. Remove the "lack of time" as an excuse and make the relationship you have with your female customer significant.

One of the best ways to create trust and an emotional connection with female customers is to create a real relationship with her. I use the word "real" with purpose; females can "feel" when someone isn't sincere, and this will chase them away. Women have higher emotional intelligence ability than men, based on common ability tests such as the Mayer-Salovey-Caruso Emotional Intelligence Test (MSCEIT) and the newer Test of Emotional Intelligence.[6]

Emotional intelligence (EI), emotional leadership (EL), emotional quotient (EQ), and emotional intelligence quotient (EIQ) are the capabilities of individuals to recognize their own emotions and those of others, discern between different feelings and label them appropriately, use emotional information to guide thinking and behavior, and manage and/or adjust emotions to adapt to environments or achieve one's goal(s).[7] Women have a stronger, more innate ability to decipher the emotions and behaviors of others, leading them to know when someone is being disingenuous much more quickly than a man does. Again, it is vital to show genuine interest when interacting with your female customers. This is the only chance you have to create a connection and to avoid her feeling uneasy. If you want to avoid this "uneasy feeling," you simply need to get to know your female consumer and create a real relationship through actively listening, showing compassion and empathy, and taking an interest in what she needs or wants (even if it's outside of purchasing!).

As you build real relationships with your female consumers and learn more about them, you should capture the golden nuggets they share with you and use them in meaningful ways to tailor and personalize your female customer's experience. Paying attention to what matters to your female consumer and then using that information to create a tailored experience shows you care about and cherish the female consumer, and demonstrates genuineness.

For example, if she comes into your business and talks about her son Johnny playing in a soccer tournament, the next time she visits your store, make sure to ask her how Johnny's soccer tournament went. Remembering this detail not only personalizes the experience, but also contributes to building a stronger relationship. Women need to feel this emotional connection. She wants the product and person who is serving her to inspire and fulfill an emotional need, not just a transactional need.

For example, the reason a man and woman (couple) want to buy a car might be very different. The man may think, "It will help me get to work and back home without the inconvenience of unreliable public transportation" (a transactional reason that fulfills a basic need), whereas the woman is thinking, "This car will help us to spend more time together and do things on the weekend" (an inclusive and interactional reason). Both needs are important, but as this demonstrates, the woman requires the brand or person serving her to "know" her so they can deliver on her emotional needs. Getting to know her and creating a real relationship are the only ways your business can deliver on her needs.

When I am shopping, I love when the sales associate takes an interest in me. While I have many favorite stores, there is one brand I always visit whenever I need a boost in my wardrobe (and self-confidence). What I love most about my experience there is how they take the time to create a genuine connection.

Once I went into the store after a very tough week. I know I have mentioned this before, but retail therapy is a thing! The sales associate asked me what I did for a living and when I told her that I was a speaker and trainer, she actually asked how she could help me become better at what I do! The conversation flowed from that point forward. While I don't think my credit card felt better afterward, I certainly did. She is now one of the few people I go back to every time I need a little boost.

I can also remember when I used to be a sales associate at Guess. I had this one customer who would come in once a week (she eventually bought out the entire store). She would arrive right as the store opened on Thursdays to check out what was new. The two of us gained such a fantastic connection that even when I moved stores, she followed! I believe Thursday mornings were much more than a shopping event for her. She craved the connection she had with the people who served her, and this loyalty to the sales associate made her in turn loyal to the brand.

Remember, she holds purchasing influence for three to four generations in her orbit, most of whom are your future customers. If you fail to establish a relationship with her, not only will you lose her as a customer, but you will also lose her referrals.

THE CONNECTION FORMULA

As you now know, women crave connections as part of our physiological makeup, and establishing a connection with your female consumer will go a long way. Unlike the male consumer, women are more likely to depend on a sales associate to provide them with the required information they need to help make their decision. Remember, a man is on a mission, but a woman is on a journey when shopping. Men know what they want and want to make the transaction as quickly as possible, whereas women want to connect, create a relationship, and enjoy the process. Your female consumer wants a relationship with the person who is serving her and will depend on that person to create the experience; that includes finding out what she wants and needs and providing her with the necessary information. You'll never uncover what information she truly needs if you don't get to know her through actively listening, asking questions, and showing genuine interest in her as a woman first. Females want to be listened to, be taken seriously, and feel a connection with you and your brand; these factors drive her decision and her loyalty to you. When you connect with someone, you bond with them, and that is the difference between a one-time purchase and loyalty.

Teaching a team how to emotionally connect and be genuine is a struggle in every organization I have worked with. To help businesses connect with female consumers, I created what I like to call "The Connection Formula." This formula is based on the research I have done around women's needs and wants, and how females go about creating a connection with another human being. The Connection Formula is a list of ways you can connect with the female consumer in an order that will promote connection and relationship building.

This checklist is designed as a training tool you can use to help raise your team's emotional intelligence and assist them in increasing their ability to create a connection with your female consumer. Women need to feel emotionally connected to your brand and the people who represent your brand. A woman wants the product and person who is serving her to inspire and fulfill an emotional need, not just a transactional need. Emotions play an important role in a woman's purchasing decisions and brand loyalty. Often, she doesn't buy a product or service because of price, quality, and value for her money. Instead her choice is driven by an emotional connection and how she feels about the brand or the person serving her.

The Connection Formula is a list of ways you can connect with the female consumer in an order that will promote connection and relationship building. The formula is also an easy way to train your team (both corporate and frontline) to gain an emotional connection with your female customers until they get the hang of it naturally; after all, women crave connection.

COMPASSION AND EMPATHY: The way to a woman's heart is through her heart! Showing compassion and empathy toward your female consumer will lead to a more trusting relationship much faster. From a brand perspective, Procter & Gamble (P&G) did an excellent job with its "Thank you, Mom" ad campaign. If you have not watched this, you should! The opening scenes show a flashback of a mother and child together, and then a flash forward to the child as an extraordinarily successful grown adult. It shows how much Mom cares for and protects her children and how much those children can achieve with their mothers by their sides. This ad is a fantastic example of how a brand can pull at a woman's heart strings by showing compassion and empathy for their role as Mom. Personally, as a mom myself, I cry every time I watch this ad. The ad closes with: "P&G, Proud Sponsor of Moms."

REVEAL VULNERABILITIES: Yes, as a company (and a leader) you must show your softer side. Displaying vulnerability lets the female consumer know that the people behind the company are human too. This doesn't mean you need to reveal your deepest,

darkest secrets through social media, or during one-on-one interactions with a customer. What it does mean is that you have to
find out where her struggle is, and if you as a person have the same
challenges as a she does, don't be afraid to let her know that you
understand where she is coming from. Listen to and uncover what
your female consumers connect with, then match what's important to her. Reveal that you, too, share similar views. Remember: it's
not about you, it's about how you connect with her and how she
feels during her interactions with you. Revealing vulnerabilities in
a brand message or through an in-person experience will go a long
way toward your brand becoming human in her eyes.

ENGAGE GENUINELY: I've mentioned this before, but the number
one reason a woman will walk away from your brand is that she doesn't
like the way she was treated. Your female consumer can sen se insin-
cerity from a mile away. If you are going to engage with your female
customers in any way, make sure you are genuine in your approach.
Part of engaging genuinely with the female consumer is to do as you
say. There is nothing more disheartening for a female consumer than
a brand that says they care, but it turns out they don't or aren't taking
the actions needed to execute on their promise. A woman will appreciate a brand that is genuine; not one that states that they care, when
in actuality they don't take any action.

Companies such as BrewDog will support women at times like
International Women's Day in their ads, yet the disparity of women
at the top or even on the sales floor is huge. I talk about this in
more depth in Chapter 7, but I feel it serves a purpose here as well.
Women connect to brands that have people who really care, not
with brands that "fake it until they make it."

ASSURE AND VALIDATE: All I ever want from my fiancé is reassurance. Heck, it's all I ever want from anyone I interact with. Women have an uncanny ability to put themselves down, compare themselves to others, and covet what they don't have. When a women shares her feelings and asks an opinion, what she really wants is assurance that her feelings, in that moment, are valid. You may be thinking, isn't that all humankind? Well, yes, but remember a woman's limbic brain is almost double the size of a man's. When she "feels" or "needs" validation, those emotions can come barreling in like a freight train without brakes (at least that's what I get told every time I need validation from my fiancé!). You must assure your female customer that her thought process is on the right track, validating her feelings and decision to choose you.

TAKE TIME: Anything worthwhile usually takes patience and time. As a business trying to understand the demographic, don't cut corners. As a sales associate, spend the time to get to know her and allow her the time to get to know you. The female customer doesn't want to be rushed. She wants to feel like the priority. Take your time to get to know her, and this will serve you well. Simple.

EVOLVE THE RELATIONSHIP: If we stop learning, we might as well be dead. If you stop evolving your relationships with your female customers (all customers, really), you might as well close your doors. Because without evolution of the relationship, you will not be in tune with how to tailor the experience as her needs and wants change. Your employees evolve, your customers will continue to evolve, and technology is speeding through evolution at a rapid pace. You must be agile. The female consumer will continue to move through her life stages, and if you want to stay relevant in her world, you must be open to (and work hard at) maintaining and evolving the relationship and connection you have with her. Remember that your female customer influences purchase decisions for three to four generations, and if you lose the relationship with her, you lose it with them, too. Not taking the time to evolve the relationship will cause her to make her next purchase someplace else.

Emotional connection with someone close to you doesn't always come easily, so I understand how hard it can be to connect with a stranger. Getting your team comfortable with being uncomfortable will help them to get over the fear of opening up, showing compassion, and being vulnerable with your customers. As a brand, you must become like an investigator; always look for ways you can give value to her and connect with her rather than how you can get value from her. We are all in the business of being human, interacting with humans, and creating human experiences for each other. Give women what they want—a hedonic atmosphere, and strong relationships and connections.

WOMEN ON TOP

*W*hat else do women want? The same thing that men do: the ability to advance in the workplace based on their skills and merit.

I am sure you have experienced or know about gender inequality, diversity, and the number (or lack thereof) of women sitting at the table in organizations across the world. Perhaps you're even asking yourself, "This conversation again?" Here's the thing: This conversation needs to continue to happen, not only to help the women of the world (and those in *your* world), but to improve the health and success of your organization.

In the future, the purchasing power of women around the world will keep rising, but with the lack of women in top positions, decisions will continue to be made by men, delivered by men, for men. Persisting to lead in this manner will significantly reduce female loyalty to traditionally male-dominated industries and businesses, which will mean losses of retention, referrals, and revenue. Considering that the female consumer influences between 80 and 90 percent of household purchases, having a strong female presence in your workplace and at an executive level will, without a doubt, ultimately attract female consumers to your brand.

THE STARK REALITY

As I've mentioned, female executives account for less than 20 percent of executives across the world. According to a study conducted by McKinsey & Company, women make up an average of just 21 percent of the members of executive teams in the United States, 12 percent in the United Kingdom, and 6 percent in Brazil, while remaining underrepresented at the top of corporations globally.[1]

LinkedIn reviewed over 300 million profiles and revealed some pretty startling facts as well. In the last decade, the percentage of women in the workplace has grown by only 4 percent, and in another study, it was revealed that women account for only 39 percent of all sales staff in the United States.[2] I remember feeling overwhelming shock at some of the statistics I found while researching the female consumer in relation to women in the workplace.

Curious to know what growth has been evident in my thirty-five years of life, I looked back to my birth year, 1984. I found that in the United States that year, only 37 percent of all women between the ages of twenty and sixty-four, and 41 percent of all women between the ages of twenty-five and forty-four, held full-time, year-round jobs (including teaching jobs). Comparing that to where the world stands right now, thirty-five years later, the progressive climb has been at a snail's pace. Men currently hold 62 percent of manager-level positions, while women hold just 38 percent.[3] The number of women decreases at every subsequent level of management.

We have essentially stood still in regard to gender diversity in the workplace. While the standstill could be a reflection of the choices women are making, it's also undeniable that tenacious discrimination is one of the top reasons why women are not entering the workforce in greater numbers. Women are, on average, 30 percent less likely to be called for a job interview than men with the same qualifications.[4] Not only is it hard for women to move up in the ranks, it is a challenge to even get our foot in the door; even if we have the same qualifications!

What makes my mind explode is how beneficial it is to the top line of businesses to have diversity in the workplace, yet there are still unnecessary and overlooked opportunities to bring women up through the ranks.

According to Lean In's "Women in the Workplace" research, females continue to be underrepresented at every level, and as the 2021 study revealed, women are less likely to be hired and promoted to managers. While the number of women in executive roles has grown slightly over the last few years, the number of women in entry-level management positions has remained stagnant, which tells us that there are fewer women to promote into more senior positions.[5]

The 2019 "Women in the Workplace" study also shows that it is possible to increase gender diversity in the workplace if business leaders simply hire and promote women at the same rate as men. If male (and female!) leaders did that, America could add one million more women to corporate management over the next five years.

If the sheer injustice of it all isn't enough to seek change, a business's bottom line and brand reputation will only benefit by improving and diversifying your hiring and promotional practices. When women want (and get the opportunity) to work and grow with an organization, female consumers will take notice and support those organizations with their influence and purchasing power. That means brand preference and loyalty for your company, which results in growing profits. Simple.

GENDER DIVERSITY YIELDS HIGHER PROFITS

In my research, I have read over and over again how organizations have little to no understanding of how to market or serve the world's largest consumer demographic. The funny thing is, women have been consumer-based organizations' largest customer segment as far back as the 1800s. The problem is that very few companies are willing to acknowledge the spending power the female consumer has because it requires them to put thought and effort into designing experiences outside of their comfort zone. Even fewer are eager to take the time to understand the decision maker or hire people who do.

The McKinsey study also revealed that companies in the top quartile for gender diversity are 15 percent more likely to have financial returns above their respective national industry medians. On the flip side, the study shows that companies in the bottom quartile for gender, ethnic, and racial diversity are statistically less likely to achieve above-average financial returns than the average companies in the data set (that is, bottom-quartile companies are lagging, rather than merely not leading).[6] Achieving diversity is not easy, because if it were, it would have been achieved. However, realizing diversity is necessary, given that increased diversity yields growth, profit, and higher returns. The time to invest in gender diversity is now; be the business that pulls ahead of the pack and reaps the rewards.

Just as important, women understand women, so who better to design an experience for the decision maker than a woman? Hiring and advancing more women to the top will only benefit a company's ability to understand the world's most influential consumer and design an experience in which she wants to partake! Having women at the helm is like having a ringer on the inside, allowing your company to get the scoop into what women want. Of course, even females need to pay attention to the research about what their specific customers want, need, and desire. Even women can't simply guess because they're females too; but being a woman can certainly bring a certain insider advantage.

The conversation about female equality or gender diversity will continue; it's up to you whether or not you want to move into action and make a difference in the experience you provide to the female decision maker. A female lens in your organization will not only increase your financial returns as women continue to take over spending power in every aspect of life and business, but will also contribute to higher customer satisfaction among your female consumer base. This satisfaction will yield higher profits through conversation, referrals, and loyalty.

TAKING ACTION

I wrote an article called "Inspiration Just Isn't Enough!" that outlined the vast gender gap in the automotive industry (one of the most male-dominated industries that exists), and how inspirational words about how gender diversity means something to them just weren't going to cut it. If you want to make a difference, you have to *be* the difference.

The definition of insanity is "to do the same thing over and over again and expect a different outcome."

If we were to put many of the male-dominated industries like automotive, finance, and medical up against this definition, it is clear as day that those industry leaders are insane! These industries are all hoping to reach profitable female consumers and reduce the gender gap in the workplace, yet their leaders are not making the necessary changes in order to achieve these results.

No one is going to come with a magic wand and cast a spell that makes any of these male-dominated industries (especially automotive dealers and original equipment manufacturers) the top place to work for females or a place where female consumers feel comfortable. Leaders in these industries must choose to do something different and enact the changes necessary to see a different outcome. Now is the time to stop the insanity.

As a business leader, you can work to create a network of tools, resources, and pathways that support women in the industry to grow without worrying about the glass ceiling that has been above their heads for decades. These pro-female programs will help bring more women into the workforce and keep them there.

"If you build it, she will come."

Many industries have struggled with inclusivity for women. Women represent approximately 19 percent of the retail automotive workforce (depending on which study you look at). Automotive isn't alone in this—there are other historically male-dominated industries that are in the same proverbial boat as far as breaking through the "boys' club" mentality. Technology and finance have just as much trouble as automotive. Isn't it time to break the script and hire for diversity, knowing the impact women have, not only on businesses as consumers but within an industry's internal culture? It is imperative that we start creating cultures that are conducive to women. The fact is that people want to buy from brands they can relate to—where they see a reflection of their own lives. That means that your female customer will want to see women working for you!

GM IS BREAKING THE CYCLE

The automotive industry is a traditionally male-dominated one; however, one brand is taking significant steps in the right direction.

In 2013, Mary Barra became General Motors' chairman and Chief Executive Officer—the first female CEO of a major global automaker.

Since taking the helm at GM, she has made it her mission to build a strong culture for females in the automotive industry. "Corporate culture doesn't change quickly, but it's critical to have a strong culture to motivate employees and to cultivate an environment that breeds success."[7, 8]

GM established the GM Women's Retail Network, which offers forums and development courses to women, and promotes men and women working together.

Recently, GM has also developed three core values for the company: "The Customer Is Our Compass," "Relationships Matter," and "Individual Excellence Is Crucial."

Having core values like these is a step in the right direction to attracting female candidates and ultimately female consumers; these values outline that people come first, decisions are made with the individual in mind, and culture matters. Having this focus makes GM a very approachable automotive brand to the female consumer. Women take notice of the headlines and will gravitate toward the brands that support and empower other women.

GM seems to understand the fact that if women want to work for them, female consumers are more apt to buy from them. That's why they're breaking the script!

What can *you* learn from GM?

I believe that your happiest customer is only as happy as your happiest employee, and the gender diversity you support within your organization plays an important role in how your employees treat their customers.

As our employment environment and the needs of our internal customers change, organizations have to be willing to put systems in place to attract, hire, train, and retain more female employees. Although companies are gradually adding more women at a C-suite level, there is still disparity and we are nowhere close to providing equality. Given the critical role top executives play in shaping the business and culture of their company, if you add one woman to the top echelon of your company, your workplace culture will positively feel the difference.

I believe diversity and inclusion will become more and more important as Generation Z moves into the workforce. This generation does not see gender—or color, for that matter—in the same way that perhaps Gen Xers saw it before them. Change seems to be the only constant, and we must move with our shifting workforce or get left behind. Companies today must show that they are creating a safe space in which all genders and races can be successful.

SPONSORSHIP

Besides the lack of advancement past the entry-level management position, there is another reason women are not advancing into executive roles at the same pace as men. That reason is due to a lack of leaders willing to sponsor highly qualified women by speaking up on their behalf, ensuring the appropriate stepping stones for women to advance. A sponsor is integral in the climb to the top. A sponsor is someone with influence who is willing to use that influence to support an employee and promote the employee's skills and abilities. Unfortunately, sponsors tend to lean toward like individuals—men with men—and because there are still more men at the table, women lose out here, too. Women have to fight even harder to gain traction with a female sponsor, because there are fewer of them.

THE BROKEN RUNG: INEQUALITY
IN HIRING AND ADVANCEMENT

According to the Women in the Workplace study conducted by the Lean In organization, the biggest obstacle women face on the path to senior leadership is at the first step up to manager. For every one hundred men who are promoted or hired as managers, only seventy-two women are promoted and hired. This broken rung results in more women getting stuck at the entry level and fewer women becoming managers. Not surprisingly, men end up holding 62 percent of manager-level positions, while women hold just 38 percent.[9]

This early inequality has an enormous impact on the advancement of women into executive positions. If there are fewer women up for the promotion, then there will be fewer opportunities to take a seat at the table. More women in management positions will not only close the gender gap but will greatly improve the experience your female consumers are receiving, meaning that your company's bottom line will flourish.

EIGHT

THE MERITS OF A FEMALE-FRIENDLY WORKPLACE CULTURE

f women don't enjoy working for you, why would they want to shop or buy from you?

Even today, female-friendly workplace cultures are still scarce. You should be aware that the culture you foster within your business is a direct reflection of the ease and comfort of your customers. It is in the best interest of your company to build a culture that women can get behind. If you do this, both female employees and consumers will take notice!

Do you want to offer an experience *she* can't live without? Then you'd better create a culture where women want to work. The ultimate effect is that women feel comfortable buying from you. As the saying goes, happy wife, happy life. This is the same for your organization: happy female employees, happy female consumer, happy company (and higher profits!).

One of my favorite people on planet Earth is my friend Sandy, an

HR expert who focuses on creating diversity in the automotive industry. She knows a thing or two about fighting her way to the top of an industry ruled by men. Sandy and I have had many conversations on the topic of cultivating an experience-driven culture in the workplace, and she says, "People are the heart of any organization, and I've long had a firm belief that creating loyalty, true engagement, and positive experiences for our *internal* customers leads to creating the sought-after customer-for-life, and as a result—increased profits. Study after study shows that companies that foster an environment of engagement for their employees see a 20 percent increase in productivity! So why aren't all companies doing this? Why aren't we all treating our employees like the valued internal customers that they are? And why—*why*—are companies in many industries ignoring almost half of the workforce—women? These are really the big questions."

She couldn't be more accurate.

These questions have been plaguing me for years, which brings me right back to my argument at the top of this chapter: If women don't enjoy working for you, why would the female consumer want to shop with you? Cultivating a culture that encourages and supports women will only increase engagement from your employees and your customers. It is a win-win.

Encourage a culture where women are equal and are thought of as equals, and your team will view them as equals. If your team treats each other with the same (if not better) experience as your customers, your customers will feel it.

There are challenges women face in the workforce that most men do not; these challenges need to be illuminated and reflected in the workplace culture. Let's take a look at some of the biggest issues that need to be addressed in a female-friendly workplace culture.

EQUAL PAY

How is this still a challenge? We are all humans with skills, knowledge, passion, and drive to succeed. Why is it that women are continuing the fight for equal pay? Women wake up just like men, get ready for work, and arrive on time. They work hard, complete their assignments, lead their teams all in the same fashion (sometimes better) than their male counterparts, yet women are paid 79 cents on the dollar in comparison to their male colleagues, and it's even worse for women of color.[1] If the person is skilled enough to have the job and they deliver, then they shouldn't be paid less because of their gender or nationality. Period.

RACE AND GENDER BIAS

Bias impacts women every day at the workplace. Women of color continue to deal with some of the workplace's most entrenched hurdles. Thirty-three percent of women and 11 percent of men say they have seen or heard biased behavior toward women. According to Lean In's "Women in the Workplace" 2019 research, black women and women with disabilities face more barriers to advancement and get less support than other groups of women.[2]

Worse yet, 73 percent of women reported experiencing discrimination in the form of microaggressions, which have been rooted in bias. Microaggressive behavior consists of brief but daily verbal, behavioral, or environmental indignities. Mistaking a female physician for a nurse or assuming someone is dangerous or a criminal because of their race are simple but very real examples of what microaggressive behaviors look like. These outbursts can be intentional or unintentional but are classified the same way regardless. Behavior like this communicates hostile, derogatory, or negative prejudicial slights and insults toward culturally marginalized groups and can be very damaging to the workplace culture. The problem is that discrimination or bias often goes unnoticed because both the victim and the coworker who witnesses it stay silent. Only about a third of employees who've seen bias over the past year spoke up personally to challenge it—and less than a quarter say someone else did. Less than half of men in the workplace and only 32 percent of women believe that disrespectful behavior toward women is often quickly addressed by their company.[3] Stats like this clearly demonstrate the uphill battle women still face in the workplace as they fight for equality.

SEXUAL HARASSMENT

Over the last few years, sexual harassment against women in the workplace has become a topic of conversation and concern. According to an article written in *Inc.* magazine, 60 percent of women say they experience "unwanted sexual attention, sexual coercion, sexually crude conduct, or sexist comments" in the workplace.[4] Sexual harassment affects women at all levels within an organization, and this greatly affects workplace engagement. Sexual harassment has a multitude of negative effects on the victim. Some include negative mood, eating disorders, alcohol abuse, job withdrawal, greater stress, greater self-doubt, lower self-esteem, and lower overall mental health.[5] How can women climb their way to the top if they don't feel safe in the environment in which they work? This is a challenge no person should face.

Regardless of what the challenge is, the reality is that women face completely different types of problems than men do. It's unfortunate, and I hope this reality will change. If leaders recognize the need for change, it will. Brands who are behind the times in creating equality for their female employees are probably also way behind when it comes to identifying the importance and impact the female consumer has on their business.

THE CHALLENGE: WHAT WILL YOU DO
TO IMPROVE YOUR CULTURE?

When you want to achieve something bigger and better, you must be willing to change yourself fundamentally. You must be willing to become intentional and deliberate with everything you do. If you want true transformation, you must start by strengthening the core of who you are and what you expect, then do what's needed to become stronger. The sayings, "What you put out is what you get back," and "You are a mirror reflection of yourself" are very true.

Achieving something better will strengthen your profits, your brand image, and your personal ethics. Making your workplace culture more amenable to female employees can bring about all of these changes. You can do this in many ways, but the next few pages offer some ideas that have been proven to work effectively because women thrive under these conditions and with these perks.

I have outlined the importance of why you want to have women working for you and leading your people. I have showed you the positive impact they can have on your top line if you clear a path for them. I have even outlined the obstacles on the path to the rise of women in the workplace. You know that your female consumer will trust your brand at a higher level if they see women like themselves represented at all levels in the organization, but the question that may be swimming around in your head (making you feel dizzy) is, "How do I attract more women, and once I have hired them, how do I retain them and keep them engaged?" I won't pretend to be an HR expert, but I have done quite a bit of research on this subject and I don't want to leave you hanging without a little "how to."

Here are eight items I advise organizations to pay attention to or change so they can transform their culture to focus on the importance of attracting, hiring, and retaining female employees.

1. *Accept that women are different than men.*

Men are simply physiologically different from women. We have reviewed the many ways men and women differ physiologically. There is no hiding from the fact that we are different. Why not accept it and use these differences to our advantage? You must fill your teams with those that have different strengths than you. When you curate teams that are filled with "like people" (people that are just like you), you won't get very far. It may be easier and feel safer to lead like people (men hiring men rather than women), but I can promise you it won't advance your agenda and success. Be open to hiring the best person with the strengths that are needed to fill the gaps on your team, regardless of gender or race. Keep in mind that women have more compassion, have a higher ability to make connections between larger concepts, have better memories, and are better at creating long-standing relationships. Accept these differences—heck, even embrace them—because they are not going anywhere.

2. *Decide that diversity is important and make it a company initiative.*

MacKay CEO Forums is a membership program in which CEOs and top executives from different businesses throughout Canada come together to learn from their peer group how to improve their skill levels as executives. A woman founded MacKay CEO Forums, and recently, I had the pleasure of discussing with her MacKay's goal of ultimately getting their membership up to 50 percent female. She wanted to achieve equality within the next two years. I suggested to her that MacKay open up the forums to women in entry management positions, so it can nurture these young women's careers and help them open the doors to the C-suite. Currently, the organization is standing at 33 percent female members, and closing this gap is a primary focus over the next couple of years. MacKay Forums recognizes the importance of advancing women in the workplace, and the company is willing to be open-minded to achieve this goal.

This is a great example of a company that has decided to make equality a focus. Without this first step of actively striving for change—if it isn't important to you as a leader or brand—the rest will simply fall through the cracks. Your brand will continue doing more damage, breaking trust with both your female employees and consumers. If you or your company haven't embraced a female-friendly workplace up until now, that's okay. Own it, and from this point forward, do a stellar job at creating a culture in which women want to work. Decide to make equality a priority and get the entire company to rally around this idea.

3. Get employees to buy into diversity.

In order for diversity to truly become part of your DNA, every person *must* believe in this. All your hiring managers must look past gender and race. All leaders must believe in equal opportunity and every frontline employee must believe that success and movement are possible. By making equality a priority and setting goals to bridge the gap, you will show your organization that this is in fact an initiative that isn't going away. A culture shift must happen, and your people must get on or get off the train. Much like designing and implementing a brand experience program, you will have those who are excited, those who sit on the fence, and those who want nothing to do with it. When you decide to put a program like this into place, you must be willing to make the hard calls to remove anyone who doesn't buy in. Because if you don't, you are sending a message to the rest of your employees that you don't actually care about transforming the culture (or experience) for either your female employees or customers. Talk about the importance of diversity at every opportunity. Share stories of success and don't let a few bad apples ruin it for the rest.

4. *Rethink the benefits your company offers.*

Identify what female candidates need or want in order to work for you, then instead of documenting these and forgetting them, do something about it. Adjust the benefits you offer your employees. Rethinking the benefits of your company won't just elevate the experience for your female employees, but for the men as well.

Flexibility is important today. Most of the time, both people in a relationship are working, which makes it even harder to raise a family and balance life in general. Single parents out there are juggling so many balls that they don't know how they will keep up. Mothers are the primary—or sole—earners for 40 percent of households with children under eighteen, according to the Department of Labor in the United States.[6] Work-life balance and flexibility is a challenge that holds major importance for mothers and their chosen employers. These women will seek out companies that support their ability to balance their lives, personally and professionally.

A few benefits to consider are flexible work hours, a work-from-home option, increased personal days, contributions to kids' college funds, mentorship programs, career advancement programs, on-site childcare, and women's groups, to name a few. Create a network of tools, resources, and pathways that support women in the industry to grow without worrying about the glass ceiling that has been above their heads for decades.

Other programs to consider are—

- Employee resource groups for women that support women in the current workplace environment
- Female-driven peer groups
- Education for personal development and career succession planning
- Mentoring programs that connect other male and female executives with up-and-coming female team members

Programs like these will help bring more women into the workforce and keep them there.

Here is a tip that I give all the companies I work with when designing a benefit program for women: Ask the women who already work for you what they want! Involve them. Ask your female employees what benefits would help them feel more cared for, balanced, and productive. While you are doing this, ask them what they would like to experience as a female customer (two birds, one stone!). The women of your company will feel as if you care about their opinions and will give you great insight. It's a win-win. If you are going to do this, however, make sure you are ready and willing to move their suggestions into action. Because if you don't, you risk losing the trust of your female employees.

5. *Set a goal for getting more women into first-level management.*

There is definitely a bottleneck of women in the promotion funnel in organizations around the world. *This has to be a focus.* Without setting a goal, you will never work toward it. Ask yourself, "How many women do I want to see at every level?" Just like MacKay Forums, who set a 50 percent female-member goal, you could do the same for gender diversity within your office. The first step to achieving gender diversity at the top is to start nurturing diversity at entry-level positions. Celebrity Cruises is another great example of an organization that supports and has achieved great strides toward equality. According to Celebrity, just 2 percent of the world's mariners are women. But they're leading the way to change that and create a more diverse future in the industry. In just four years, Celebrity has boosted the number of women working across their fleet from 3 percent to 22 percent.[7] Their goal is to bridge the gap in a big way, by bringing gender equality to the seven seas. Celebrity made a goal to have an all-female bridge and officer team sailing the world's most revolutionary ship by spring of 2020, and they made this objective a reality. Make quality a focus, set a goal, and break gender barriers in your company.

6. *Create a supportive culture that empowers employees to speak up.*

Building and maintaining a safe environment in which women feel comfortable airing their concerns will advance your equality focus at rapid speed. Much like looking to your female employees for ideas on how to change the culture and experience for themselves, future candidates, and female consumers, creating a supportive and safe culture in which women feel empowered to speak up will only benefit you and your brand. You can't fix what you don't know is broken, right? Give your female employees an outlet to speak up without repercussions. I have discussed trust a few times throughout this book. The reason why trust is so important is because without it not a single relationship would survive. That means the relationship with your female employees as well. If they keep problems to themselves, it will affect their output and ultimately your brand's success. I cited that it takes twelve positive interactions to make up for just one negative interaction with your female consumers, and this is the same for your employees. If you don't create a culture that is supportive of women speaking up, they will silently trust you less and your brand will suffer.

7. *Review your job descriptions for culture, mission, qualifications, and language.*

Now that you have decided that diversity is important, you have identified the benefits you need to offer, and your team is on board with diversity and creating a supportive culture, it's time to adjust all your hiring resources to reflect this cultural transformation. Don't keep this a secret! Shout it from the mountaintops for all potential candidates (and consumers) to hear!

Women (and men) are looking for a job with purpose, especially the new generations moving up in the workforce. They want to know they can impact the lives of their customers, the brand they work for, the coworkers they interact with daily, and the charities the brand supports. Employees also want to know that the brand they work for supports a culture they can see themselves happily working in. A job description should be more of an inspirational advertisement about your brand rather than a list of duties. The job description should show your future candidate how their role can make a difference, and not just be a list of ingredients.

The qualifications you put on your job descriptions can also impact the number of women that apply for the position. You must think long and hard about what is really required for the role and then be creative about how you decide to communicate the requirements. Remember, men and women are different. We process information differently and the perceptions we hold on the same topic can be vastly different. Research shows that when men look at a list of requirements, they feel confident enough to apply if they satisfy about 60 percent of the items. Women, on the other hand, only feel confident enough to apply if they meet closer to 100 percent of the qualifications.[8] How you outline what needs to be done to get their foot in the door will affect the number of female candidates you have applying for the position.

Finally, take one last look at the language used. Women react to a different type of language then men. There are certain words in job descriptions that can unintentionally discourage women from applying. For example, words that describe a sales position from the perspective of a hunter—hungry and aggressive—don't resonate with a female candidate. A woman doesn't want to kill, eat, or pressure a potential customer. Women are expert relationship builders and want to be able to embrace our feminine side while doing this. Females want to partner with their clients, guide them through the sales process, consult, and be trusted advisors. Women want to improve their clients' lives and build connections with others on their team, so in order to attract female candidates, use words and phrases such as "create relationships," "earn trust," "inspire change," "be bold," "help others," "collaboration," "communication," "love for the industry," and "advise." Paying attention to these details can make all the difference in attracting qualified females to your company.

8. *Get your women to share their stories.*

Take a more personalized approach. Get your women talking, and talking publicly (even on video) about all the things your brand does to embrace diversity and equality. This will be the most outward way to attract not only top female candidates but also a broader female consumer base. Kindra Hall, an expert storyteller helps individuals and companies capture attention, close more sales, and blow up their brands through the fine art of strategic storytelling. Kindra says, "People are naturally attracted to stories, they're memorable, and hearing them causes chemical changes in our brains that improve our focus and heighten our empathy."[9]

Stories create a shared experience, without the listener even realizing that they are putting themselves in the narrative. When your female employees share their stories, you will allow future candidates to experience the work environment and culture before they even interview with your company.

People work for people, not brands. Getting your employees to share their stories will connect your brand with people who will connect with your people. Women want to see other women happily working for the brand in which they are interested. From an external customer perspective, people—especially women—want to do business with people, not corporations.

By having females within the company share their stories, brands will tap into genuine emotion, which will create a connection with both your female candidates and customers. If your brand has female-positive stories to tell, tell them. Women will listen intently to the opinions, stories, and feelings of other women! Plus, women thrive on sharing these experiences because they are highly emotional creatures who care very deeply about the happiness of those around them. Not only will you attract other females into the workplace, you'll make your current female employees feel appreciated and helpful. You have your own brand ambassadors waiting in the wings; you have a megaphone to tell the world's most influential consumer that you support equality in the workplace and by extension, them. Use your social reach to gather a following by creating an emotional connection. Help them fall in love with your people through the stories your employees share.

However you decide to transform your culture, realize that it is a big undertaking but is well worth the effort. My advice? Take it one step at a time, but decide you want to make the shift. This will attract more female employees to your company, thereby attracting (and keeping) more loyal, female consumers to your brand.

NINE

BECOMING EMOTIONALLY CHARGED

*T*his advice could be the most important in generating a positive culture for women on your team *and* for attracting female consumers, which is a win-win, right? By deliberately hiring team members with high EQs—a person's emotional quotient or emotional intelligence—you can assure that these employees will be able to execute everything you implement from these pages with much more ease. Without EQ, creating a real relationship with your female consumers and a tailored experience become very tough.

WHAT IS EQ?

On a very high level, EQ is all the good stuff, like having self-awareness, listening skills, and empathy. Emotional intelligence is having the capacity to blend thinking and feeling to make optimal decisions—something critical to building your sales to women. Employees with high EQs can read people's nonverbal cues and adjust their approach based on the needs of each consumer.

I am not an EQ expert, and this book is not meant to teach you the in-depth knowledge that is out there on EQ. What these pages should do is open your mind to the thought of adding EQ into your employee hiring, onboarding, and training standards.

It's important to have the skills and knowledge to do the job; however, your employees also need EQ skills to reach female consumers (and to work effectively with coworkers!). One of the top reasons women walk away from a purchase is because they don't like the way they were approached or treated. Those with high EQ can remedy the situation and fine-tune their method.

Although the world is slowly moving away from attracting and hiring men at the top and toward hiring more women managers, as well as customer service–focused employees, the change isn't happening fast enough to keep up with the increased expectations of your female consumers.

The only way to combat this is to train for EQ!

If you are in an industry that is unattractive to women applying for work, then training (and hiring) for EQ is your best bet for attracting and positively interacting with female employees, and creating more positive moments when interacting with your customers, especially the female consumer. The importance of having high emotional intelligence skyrockets when women are involved, as we are wired to care more; remember, our limbic brains are almost double the size of a man's.

HOW DO YOU TRAIN FOR EQ?

Women are more emotionally charged than men—that is fact—and if you want to earn her business you must train your team to lead with their hearts. Author and speaker Simon Sinek teaches that decisions are based off of emotions rather than facts. The result you want is a fact—it is the outcome—but this will not inspire action or a change of behavior. If you focus on the outcome and not on the action that gives you the outcome, your team will have a hard time delivering a new skill. You must focus on *why* the skill is important to master, and how to master it. Human beings are emotional creatures, and understanding the emotional drive behind why they need to develop a new skill will evoke an emotional reaction that will inspire your team to move into action.

The best way to change a habit and create sustainability is through experiential training. (Actually, psychologists say that humans rarely take on new behaviors past the age of sixteen unless they experience a significant emotional event.) Traditional training in a classroom, didactical lectures, or even e-training does not provide learners with a high enough emotional impact, which means the knowledge learned through most training comes and goes like the ocean tide.

One of my favorite sayings that I use *all* the time during my training sessions is, "I know Monday will come," meaning we will go back to our routines, step onto our proverbial hamster wheel, and not change a thing. We'll keep doing what we've always done; leaning into what our parents, teachers, leaders, and other role models in our youth have taught us to do. However, I have figured out that there is a way to awaken our senses and provide experiential training that has an emotional impact!

CONNECTING THE DOTS

After finishing a keynote on "How to Deliver a Five-Star Experience" at a spa and esthetics conference, I chose to capitalize on the fact that my entire team was in one spot. We are a remote company, which makes meaningful training extremely difficult. With excitement, I decided to *"carpe momento"* and rounded them up when the meeting room had emptied, saying to them, "If you're going to train on how to deliver a five-star experience, you need to experience what five-star is." So off we went to visit one of the most iconic hotels known for its five-star experience: the Ritz-Carlton. As a bonus, I had a client with me, so I brought her along for the experience.

We ate at the restaurant within the Ritz, and as the meal and service progressed, I asked the team what they saw, felt, and observed. It was magical to see my team and client connect the dots of theory into practice. We focused on all the details it truly takes to deliver an experience that is thoughtful, seamless, and memorable. I watched their eyes light up every time they noticed a little detail that made a *big* difference.

One particular moment comes to mind from that night. Everyone who knows me knows that I love a glass of rosé at the end of a long day. Naturally, I proceeded to sift through the wine list for a dry rosé. Unfortunately, there wasn't a rosé by the glass on the menu. Our server that night didn't miss a beat. In true Ritz-Carlton fashion, when I asked if they had a dry rosé by the glass, she said absolutely and proceeded to tell me all of the rosé options. I asked to try a certain one and she said, "Of course." Here's the thing: She could've stopped there and just given me the option I requested. Instead, she listened to the description of what I was looking for and when she returned to give me the taste of the rosé I had requested, she also brought a bottle of Whispering Angel (my fave!). With excitement and passion, she presented the bottle and said, "I went looking to see if we had anything else that would suit your palate, and I found a bottle of Whispering Angel. It is dry and crisp and really fits with what you were looking for. Would you like a glass of this?" Of course, I said yes!

My team and client were watching the whole interaction, and once the server left, everyone beamed and began talking at once. They pointed out everything she'd done, and in that moment they saw exactly what a five-star experience provides. I was able to turn everything they had learned into reality through experiential training. They revealed the importance of the greet, the use of names, and how her attentive behavior and personalized actions led to each of them feeling cared for during the experience. Even more impactful was the excited emotions they felt while they observed and listened.

THE DIFFERENCE

Not only did they experience the difference between a regular experience and a five-star experience, they described the difference, and felt the difference. They walked away with stories to tell, which sparked an emotional event. This in turn has them living and teaching what they have learned in theory and translating it to something they'd experienced.

I do this during my workshops and trainings as well. I was recently with a group for a two-day workshop. Day one was focused on the theory behind cultivating a five-star experience and day two was focused on experiencing and building a five-star experience. I had part of the team shop their own retail locations and the other shopped competitors. This really opened up their minds and helped them to see the "theory" in action. The result was amazing! The team was engaged, energized, and excited to make their experience the best in the retail industry.

I am not the only one doing this; however, there are only a select few that do. Surprise! Ritz-Carlton is in that prestigious group. How can they expect their teams at all levels around the world to deliver a world-class experience if they don't know what it is? Each employee has the opportunity to stay one weekend at a Ritz-Carlton with their family so they can feel what it's like to experience "Ladies and Gentlemen Serving Ladies and Gentlemen." Pure brilliance!

There are many ways to deliver experiential training, but if you're not doing it then you're missing out. Because Monday will come, and your team will not experience that emotional event that connects the dots between a customer's expectations and their delivery. They will continue to do as they always do.

If you want your team to action what they are learning, then flip your training and have them experience what it is they are supposed to be absorbing or delivering. You can take them all on a retreat or an outing, assign a specific company to assess, or have them document their own customer experiences and share the stories. By taking your team members out of the classroom setting and putting them into a real situation in which they can experience and feel what it is like for someone with high EQ to interact with them, you will create an emotional event that will resonate. Once you have given your team members the opportunity to do this, ask them to report back on their findings. Most important, with the new skills your team has been given, have each one describe how he or she felt and how each employee can change the way their customers feel. As you teach EQ, you must show, not tell. If you don't, your team will not realize its true impact or rewards.

ENHANCED EMOTIONAL LITERACY

When you focus your training on soft skills (EQ) and layer in the IQ (product knowledge) as you go, you will have greater buy-in and synthesis of the information. When I train a team on EQ, I focus on the following competencies: Consequential Thinking, Optimism, Compassion and Empathy, and Vulnerability. Doing this provides your team with enhanced emotional literacy and the ability to recognize customer behavioral patterns. Training in these skills will also get your team comfortable with identifying and interpreting both simple and complex feelings by frequently acknowledging recurring reactions and behaviors during interactions with customers.

CONSEQUENTIAL THINKING

Have your team practice evaluating the costs and benefits of their choices when interacting with customers. Give your team scenarios in which they can talk through the cost or benefit to reacting in particular ways. One scenario could be when a salesperson or business gives too little thought when interacting with a female consumer. Your team can then outline the cause and consumer reaction. Then have them role-play what they could have done differently to change the female customer's reaction. Making your team aware that their actions have consequences will open their eyes to paying attention to their behaviors when interacting with the female consumer. Always remember that actions have emotional reactions; women feel more deeply than men and hold on to those feelings.

OPTIMISM

Have your team practice taking the proactive perspective of hope and possibility in all situations. Positive behavior breeds positive behavior, and an optimistic outlook is the fuel to an optimistic culture. Your happiest customer is only as happy as your happiest employee. If your team can look at each interaction as an opportunity to deliver positive moments, then they will win every time.

COMPASSION AND EMPATHY

Recognizing and appropriately responding to others' emotions plays a significant role in how EQ comes full circle. Women are emotionally charged creatures, and as we've discussed, they crave connection and relationships. They want to feel cared for and important to the brand they choose to do business with. Understanding how to flip the lens, showing compassion and empathy to your female consumer, will go a long way in creating or solidifying the connection she feels to your team and the brand.

I recently began a challenge given in a book called *The Greatest Salesman in the World* by Og Mandino.[1] The challenge is to read each of ten scrolls outlined in the book three times a day for thirty days. I am currently on scroll number two, which reminds me of the importance of showing love, compassion, and empathy, even in sales. The scroll starts out by saying, "I will greet this day with love in my heart," and goes on to explain all the ways that love triumphs over fear, anger, and hate. The last paragraph states, "With love I will increase my sales a hundred-fold and become the greatest salesman. If I have no other qualities I can succeed with love alone. Without it, I will fail though I possess all the knowledge and skills of the world. I will greet this day with love, and I will succeed."

Entering every interaction in a positive way with your female consumers will yield a positive perception of your brand. Perception is reality. Your customer's experience is their reality and yours! Employees who demonstrate compassion and empathy will show your customers that your company—and brand—cares about your customer's needs over your own.

I like to have teams share their own stories with each other. It is a great eye-opener for team members to realize that everyone has a story, even your customers. Having a greater capacity to show compassion and empathy in all situations will only increase your team's ability to focus on making each other and the customer feel special.

VULNERABILITY

This is a hot topic these days and rightfully so. We have gotten so comfortable living in a social world where you only ever put your best foot forward that we are hiding the mess that makes us imperfectly perfect. When I partner with organizations, we get very comfortable with being uncomfortable. I create a safe environment where everyone feels as if his or her opinion, feelings, and suggestions matter and are relevant. This includes being comfortable with speaking up and saying what is on your mind, regardless of how uncomfortable it may be. This allows the teams' senses to be heightened and gives them the confidence to push past their fears and the stories they tell themselves in order for them to feel better. Being comfortable with getting uncomfortably vulnerable will help your team be aware of the emotions of others, promoting open communication and proactive dialogue.

At the core, emotional intelligence is something you need to own and essentially *be,* in order to truly connect with the female consumer. You can't fake this. By being smarter with feelings, you and your team will more accurately recognize emotions in yourselves and others. This knowledge will help you and your team make decisions and craft effective solutions to the customer interactions you provide each day.

Fostering EQ leads to building deeper relationships and trust with the women you do business with, and ultimately your customers will feel cared for and emotionally connected to the brand.

When you blend EQ and IQ, you will receive maximum engagement from your female consumer. The EQ skills you provide to your team members will go a long way toward turning transactional moments into interactional experiences. Magic happens when you can blend the worlds of transactions and experiences.

Invest in the magic your business delivers. Invest in your team's EQ.

TEN

TRUST, CONSISTENCY, AND ACCOUNTABILITY

*D*elivering an experience your team and customers are excited to encounter time and time again comes from being consistent in everything you do. Consistency will be what differentiates your business from your competitors'. Delivering a consistent experience builds trust with your customers, and as you now know, trust and relationships are vital to win the veto vote of the Chief Purchasing Officer.

Yet how can a customer trust a company when its own employees can't even do the same?

Consider the following.

A *Harvard Business Review* survey revealed that 58 percent of people trust strangers more than their own bosses.[1]

The Engagement Institute states that disengaged employees cost businesses as much as $500 billion every year.[2]

Highly engaged business units achieve a 10 percent increase in customer ratings and a 20 percent increase in sales.[3]

Companies that invest in employee engagement perform up to 202 percent better than companies with low engagement.[4]

Now you are probably thinking to yourself, "Where is she going with this? How did we go from consistency to trust and employee engagement?" Hang in there; it will all come full circle.

See, this is the last stop in all my trainings, whether I am working with a company to design a five-star experience for the decision maker or helping to guide a leadership team to greatness. Without your team on board, engaged and excited to enact the changes needed, and willing to hold themselves accountable when they drop the ball (because they will), you might as well take everything you've read in this book and throw it out the window.

The equation below is the glue that holds all the pieces together. In its simplest form, it is my belief in how to gain consistent results:

Trust + Accountability = Results

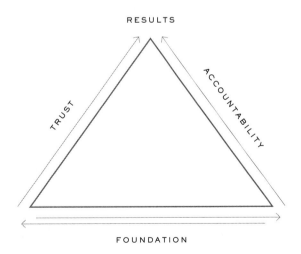

RESULTS

TRUST

ACCOUNTABILITY

FOUNDATION

You cannot gain results from your employees *or* your female consumers in any other way, period. Trust + Accountability is the foundation of any solid relationship, and together, they yield sustainable results.

Consider this question: Have you ever felt like hitting your head against the wall because you are not achieving the results you set out to achieve?

In my early days as a leader, I did. I will never forget the day my boss sat me down and said that I was the most uninspiring leader she had ever met! She shared with me that while I told my team what to do, I wasn't inspiring in them enough trust so that they *wanted* to do what I asked. As soon as I focused on earning their trust, it was much easier to hold them accountable for results.

Can you imagine what the preceding diagram would look like if trust was absent? Total chaos. When you remove trust from this tripod, everything collapses. The ability to hold your team accountable is then near-impossible; over time, they will smile and nod to your face and then turn around and not deliver on their promises. And as a result, of course, your results falter.

What do you think happens when you lose your footing on accountability, but have a team that trusts you? The same disarray.

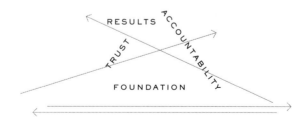

Your team members can trust you until the cows come home but what good is that if you can't hold them accountable to your expectations? We are only human, after all, and we will get busy. We will put things on the back burner when we don't feel like doing something. We will get lazy every once in a while because we are tired or decide to place blame. Maybe we think we don't have enough time or it's not our job. Do any of these excuses sound familiar? (I'm sure they do.)

If you let your team think these excuses are, in fact, reasons not to provide results, then you have lost the ability to hold your team accountable. If that is the case, you are in the same predicament as those leaders who don't have trust but think they are able to dictate results!

Bottom line: you cannot have the results you want if you don't inspire trust *and* hold your people accountable to the tasks needed to gain the expected results.

Simple, right? The concept seems basic, but earning the trust of your people and being consistent in holding them accountable (or even holding themselves accountable) is much harder to do in reality. And of course, to achieve trust and accountability with your female consumers, you must first establish trust and accountability solidly within your company.

THE TRUST SCORE

Have you ever assessed your employee trust score? I do this exercise during the discovery period with a new client and again at the end of an engagement. It is amazing to uncover what lies beneath the surface. Knowing a company's trust score gives me an immediate gauge on how successful our time together will be. I ask a very simple question.

On a scale of 0 to 10, how much do you trust your—

- Leader

- Immediate coworkers

- Other departments on which you rely

- Company as a whole

You must be open to hearing the results and be ready to action change. If you are, this can be very eye-opening and could alter the results of your organization for the better; that is, as long as you are willing to hold yourself accountable to those results and not come up with a thousand reasons or excuses as to why the result is the way it is or what can be done about it.

Once you have your trust score, you will want to chart the scores for each question on an Excel worksheet. There will be three levels to review. "Detractors" are those who mark 0 to 4; 5 to 8 are "passives"; and 9 to 10 are "promoters." You will have a bird's-eye view of your trust levels in your entire organization by doing this, which can be very revealing.

Detractors are the folks on your team who have the lowest level of trust in the company. They have no loyalty to the business, and because of this lack of trust they will leave you when the next best opportunity comes along. The detractors are also quick to play into company gossip and may be referred to as "viruses," who can negatively affect the next group: passives.

Passives have trust but their trust has been broken many times before, so they are wary. They can easily be influenced by the detractors and may partake in workplace gossip. These folks' trust can be won back with a few more deposits into their trust account.

Promoters have high trust in the company. They will sing the company's praises and advocate for company initiatives. Promoters usually won't partake in gossip unless it is to debunk the information.

Knowing your company's trust score will provide you with the insights you need to understand why initiatives may not be as successful as you thought they should be. Investing in employee engagement will help to increase your trust score and is the first step to sustained results. An increased trust score allows teams to cultivate a culture of accountability (which we will talk about next), and a culture of accountability drives results and customer satisfaction. If you want your female customers to fall in love with your brand, you must earn her trust. Consistency in the experience you provide to her is one way to do this. Start earning her business by earning the trust of your team members.

Once you have earned the trust of your people, you need to focus on how to hold them accountable to the expectations you set.

WHY IS ACCOUNTABILITY A BAD WORD?

Being accountable to the experiences you provide and the relationship you create with your female consumer will lead to a consistent experience with which she can fall in love. Unfortunately, the word *accountability* has a bad rap. Team members and brands shy away from owning their mistakes and tend to look the other way. This behavior does the opposite of what your female consumer needs your company to do; it creates inconsistency, breaks trust, and ultimately destroys the relationship she has with your brand and its people.

When I speak with a group about cultivating a culture of accountability, I begin by asking what accountability means to them. The employees usually answer with replies like these:

"It means I'm in trouble."

"Action plan."

"I am not doing a good job."

"It's annoying follow-up that goes nowhere."

Employees also say they are afraid to have conversations that hold them accountable because it means that they have to work harder.

I am amazed at how negatively the word "accountability" or the phrase "being accountable" is perceived by employees in all industries across the globe. It's no wonder organizations have a hard time committing to developing a female-specific approach. Doing that would mean companies need to be more aware, work harder, coach more, and make the necessary changes needed to make a difference. That means more effort. It's worth it, though.

As a leader, your mission should be to change the negative perception of "accountability." It is not a "bad word." Accountability can be something quite magical, and when a culture of accountability is created within an organization and is paired with a high trust score, your brand will become unstoppable—especially in your business's ability to earn her business!

When you can hold your team accountable to designing and executing an experience that women can't live without, the world's most influential consumer *will* become your brand evangelist. If you don't (or won't) hold your team accountable, the result will be inconsistency in the experience you provide or the marketing you create, which will ultimately break the trust the female consumer has with your brand. It will deter her from referring others to your brand, and will most definitely have her shopping elsewhere.

VICTIM VERSUS VICTOR

Both personally and professionally, we are the hardest on ourselves. Some of us choose to ignore the fact that our current life's circumstances are actually a direct reflection of ourselves—not the people or events that surround us. It is very comfortable and easy to take on the role of the victim, or at least it often feels that way. I can tell you, however, that every time you or your team member leans on an excuse or places blame when situations in life and business aren't favorable, they are giving their power away.

As a business, your power lies in the experience you provide to your customers. *You* have the power to take control of how your female customers perceive you. *You* can be a victor and win the hearts and minds of the Chief Purchasing Officer—if you so choose. Or you can make excuses as to why you can't, and you will never reap the benefits of her power and influence.

You cannot control the hand of cards you are dealt—the mood of the customer, the weather that affects sales, a turn in the market, or the crappy morning you had before you came into work. I know we think we have those magical powers, to control our circumstances. What we do have control of, however, is our reaction to the cards we're dealt, the team you have, and the experiences your brand provides to its consumers. You can choose to relinquish your powers by playing victim, or take your power back. Own the circumstances and be accountable to the part you play. In her eyes, that is the experience she will remember: your brand's accountability.

You will be victorious when you look in the mirror first before placing blame for any breakdown. When something fails, ask yourself, "What part did I play? What could I have done differently, and most important, what am I going to do about it to be better tomorrow than I am today?" These questions should always be applied when a customer complains or is unhappy. At the end of the day, when there is a breakdown, it may not be your fault, but it is your problem.

The key difference (and really the only difference) between very successful and unsuccessful companies, entrepreneurs, or people in life is this: They don't spend time wallowing in self-pity. They don't play victim. They *do* pull up their bootstraps, take a look at the lessons they've learned from the situation, and take control of what happens next. They take their power back instead of giving it away. Again, this seems like a very simple concept, but it is very hard to execute. If it weren't, then this world would be filled with super successful people who own their mess.

Do you have the courage to move past your fear of being part of the problem?

Nine times out of ten, we do or don't make decisions based on fear. We fear that we are not good enough, that we don't have the skill, that we will fail, or worse, that we will be called out on all of these things. We will never be fearless, but those who choose to have the courage to move past their fears are far more likely to hold themselves consistently accountable and see that being accountable is not a bad thing. They will see that pushing past their fears will not only make them stronger, but will allow them the freedom to achieve more than they ever thought was possible.

Take a minute and think about it: Do you shy away from certain things because you fear the outcome? Or maybe you fear the hard work it is going to take to correct the course of action? If the answer is no, you are lying to yourself. Now, your team is human too (the last time I checked, robots haven't completely infiltrated our day-to-day life), which means they fear hard work and potential failure. It's simply easier to make up excuses as to why you can't satisfy your female customer.

Heck, that's why a lot of companies ignore her altogether, because it's easier to forget she exists and is different (and has different expectations) than a man.

It's high time you and your team take a look in the accountability mirror, own the experience you provide, and walk through the fear of hard work, failure, or possible outcomes.

I coached a car dealership's leadership team for a few years, but when I first started working with them, they were one of the most dysfunctional groups I had ever encountered. They were broken because they came across as a group of victims that gave every excuse in the book as to why their location sat in the bottom 5 percent of their dealership group. On top of being dysfunctional in business, they were also very lost in their personal lives, which only increased the havoc in the workplace.

My hope when I work with groups like this is to change them personally. If I only focused on professional gains, the results would not be sustainable. Their habits would return, and, of course, they would go right back to where they started.

At the end of our second year of coaching them both personally and professionally, I had the team over to my house to wrap up the past twelve months and plan the year to come. When I went around the table and asked them what their biggest lesson had been over the past year, I was astonished by the answers. One leader shared that he had been on antidepressants for as long as he could remember, but because of this coaching, he realized that he has what it takes to take control of his life; he shared with us that he had been off antidepressants for three months and was feeling more alive and in control than he had ever been. Another leader shared that she realized that she deserves to be happy, and she had the power within her to make herself happy. The dealer principal shared that she needed to let go and trust her team. The last one to share was a brilliant, up-and-coming leader. She said, "I know now that I can stretch myself and I won't break. I will survive growth and hard times."

If you can cultivate a culture of accountability in your company focused on elevating the experience your team provides to each other and the female consumer, you will produce a team of victors. I promise, you will not break (even though it might feel that way). I promise you that your team and your business will only thrive, gaining customers for life in the process.

If you truly want sustainable change in your business, you must push yourself. You must get very comfortable with being uncomfortable. I can promise you that if you don't embrace accountability or earn your people's trust, you will never fully capitalize on the fruits of your labor. Again, the definition of insanity is doing the same thing over and over again and expecting a different outcome. We are all a little insane; we all live in that hamster wheel that just keeps spinning. I dare you to get off the wheel, set priorities, and take your power back. Look at your life, your business, and the experience you offer your female employees and customers, and ask yourself if you are ready to make the change. If the answer is yes, then get ready to stumble and fall. Have the courage to get back up, stretch yourself and your team, and achieve results you didn't think were possible.

BE SOLUTION FOCUSED: BUILD A BRAND FEMALES LOVE

Once you muster up the courage to take the leap in designing a brand experience your female consumers can't live without, you will need to keep yourself from stumbling back into victim mode. Naturally, you and your team will place blame or make excuses when the hard work comes into play. I mean, there is *a lot* of work to do. You have to enhance and utilize EQ skills, get your leadership excited, create consumer personas, and journey map through her eyes. You will need to develop company training, guide your leaders, then prepare your team. Last but not least, you must continue to coach your team.

A mentor of mine has taught me that when it comes to designing and executing a brand experience, you will never arrive, per se, but you can evaluate and evolve. Your brand, its people, and customers will continue to evolve, and so should the experience you provide. Your Chief Purchasing Officer will move through life stages and you will need to be ready to serve her differently. The question becomes, "Are you ready to do what it takes to be victorious in your pursuit, or are you going to fall into victim mode at the first sight of an obstacle?"

You *will* trip and fall—you will want to give up—and giving up will seem easier. However, I want you to remember that you gain power by how you react. You gain your power by focusing on what you can do differently versus what you think is supporting you. One of the best ways to remain in control is to be solution focused. A simple way to do this is to follow the age-old adage, "If you come up with a problem, then make sure you have three solutions ready!" Enforcing this simple behavior will eventually have your team coming to you with solutions. They will focus on how to solve the situation at hand rather than complaining about it. I have found the following six practices to be very impactful in up-skilling your team's problem-solving abilities.

Each of these problem-solving skills, once put into practice, will enable your team to elevate and personalize the experience they provide to the female consumer, because they will find it easier to ask and listen, see from her point of view, and find a way to build trust, relationships, and loyalty.

1. *Stay Engaged*

The moment your team members (or you!) become disengaged, there will be no passion; they will play the victims, and your results will be very hard to sustain. This is why it is so important to keep the stats I mentioned at the beginning of this chapter in mind.

- Companies that invest in employee engagement perform up to 202 percent better than companies with low engagement.
- Disengaged employees cost businesses as much as $500 billion every year.

Don't be the company that loses out. Keep your team engaged and earn the results you deserve. Give your female customer a voice at every meeting or huddle. Make her important so your team stays engaged. Staying engaged will push your team and your brand to strive consistently for excellence and look for ways to earn her business.

2. *Be Persistent*

Don't give up when you fail once, twice, three, or four times. Keep pushing. There is a solution. I was coaching an executive team on accountability, and right after one of our sessions they were put to the test. We were all sitting around the boardroom after having lunch, working through the importance of being solution focused, when a sales associate burst into the room. Frantically (and nervously), she let the group of leaders know that they were going to lose a customer *and* a million dollars as a result. I watched panic set in among the leaders. Their eyes were darting back and forth. As the alarm increased, they settled into victim mode. They started blaming everyone else as to why the customer was leaving them.

I started to chuckle, which broke the finger-pointing and blame game they were playing with each other. The president looked at me and asked, "What?" I stood up and said, "Are we going to give up? Are you going to relinquish your power and let this circumstance control you? Or are you going to take your power back and find a solution?" The tables turned and they began to focus on solving for the problem rather than being paralyzed victims. It took eight different ideas to come up with the one that solved the customer's concern, which in turn saved the client, the million-dollar order, and actually gained greater loyalty (and an additional $500,000). My role was to coach them not to give up when one solution didn't work. They had to be persistent until they thought of the right solution. It is easy to fall into victim mode. It is hard to keep going, but the reward is so much greater. You will lose your female customer's trust, her loyalty, and her buying power if you give up when the going gets tough.

3. *Think (and Do) Differently*

I will bring up the definition of insanity here once again: You cannot do the same old thing and expect a different outcome. Remember the story of the woman who learned that she could stretch herself and wouldn't break? You and your team can do the same. Try new things and get comfortable with being uncomfortable! Dare yourself to think outside the proverbial box, especially when you are coming up with solutions. It may not feel natural to look at both sexes and their physiological differences; it may be out of the norm to do the work and break down the journey through her eyes. The most successful brands have done just that. They looked beyond the tip of their noses and got comfortable with being uncomfortable. The female consumer's power and influence will only grow; by not pushing past your comfort zone, you will miss out on the rewards that come from living up to her expectations.

4. *Create New (Positive) Habits*

We are pretty hardwired by the age of sixteen. Our habits have set in and they are difficult to change unless we undergo an emotional event. Creating new habits goes hand in hand with daring to think and do differently. When you have positive habits, being solution-driven becomes much easier. It was often thought that it took twenty-one times of repeating (or not repeating) the same action to make or break a habit. Yet new research shows that with wide-reaching social media, the modern need for instant gratification, and the fact that our attention is being pulled in more directions than ever before, it now takes sixty-six days of repeating (or not repeating) an action to make or break a habit.[5] But don't give up on creating new, positive habits. Consistency will set you apart and cultivate a trust with your female consumer. Get good at creating new (and positive) habits that you can sustain.

5. *Take the Initiative*

Nike says it best: Just do it! I mean, what are you waiting for? I was having a conversation with a fellow author. He wanted my opinion on his new book idea. I thought it was brilliant. He started by telling me that in his experience, when you make a decision to do something, "things" start happening. He continued to say that most of us stand still because we are either waiting for someone else to do something for us or we are fearful of taking action. I couldn't agree more! When cultivating a culture of accountability and curating an elevated experience, you must be willing to be the one that makes the decision and moves into action. You can't wait for anyone else to change what you have the power to change. Take the initiative to try something new, come up with solutions, and take your power back. Then you can reap the benefits the female customer will bring you.

6. *Stay Curious*

Last but not least on my list of solution-driven skills is to stay curious. Be a student. Ask questions, be open to new ideas and best practices. Your team (and the people in your life) are full of them. Encourage your team to read articles and books and share what they have learned. Doing this will broaden the scope from which you can draw solutions. I guess that's why they say knowledge is power!

You hold the power to rise above your circumstances and get the results you want or need in life and business. Ask yourself: Are you willing to do what it takes to get those results? Are you willing to hold yourself accountable, consistently look for new solutions, and action the changes needed to be successful? We all have the ability to do this, and *you will not break.* It's all about the will to do it.

Trust + Accountability = Results. Earn *her* trust, hold your team accountable, and watch the results happen.

ELEVEN

A MESSAGE FOR THE LADIES (AND GENTLEMEN)

I've written a lot about how leaders should change their hiring practices to encourage gender diversity, promote more women to higher positions, and encourage a female-friendly workplace culture. Now what can you do, as a woman, to bust into the boys' club and make your way to the top? After all, you're a company's secret weapon for reaching their most influential consumer: the female buyer. Realize that you're a huge asset for a brand that wants to increase profits by reaching the Chief Purchasing Officer. Let them know that you can use your savvy and insider knowledge to brand to women. Sell yourself.

When I am mentoring young women who are on the rise professionally (and even personally), I emphasize that we, as females, are the only ones in control of our actions. At the end of the day, we can control whether or not our fears dictate our advancement. We can decide if we will let others' actions speak for us or if we will stand tall and speak up for ourselves. I know that women are faced with enormous hills to climb and these hills present challenges that most men will never experience, but that doesn't mean you should use it as an excuse not to get where you want to go.

I dare you to **Be Bold, Be Different, Be YOU!**

One cold November afternoon, I had just walked out of a Toastmasters meeting. Toastmasters is an awesome group that gets together to improve their public speaking skills. Being a keynote speaker was a dream of mine, and so I attended those meetings to hone my skills. I was starting my car when my phone rang. It was one of my mentors, and I remember being excited to pick up and have an energizing conversation. Unfortunately, that wasn't what was in store for me. In a serious tone, he said, "Katie, I wanted to talk to you about your chances of making it in a male-dominated industry (the speaking and consulting industry)."

Of course, I was open to hearing any feedback, so I said, "Okay, go for it."

He continued. "Well, first, you don't speak up enough when you're in group settings, and . . . well . . . you're just too young and pretty to be taken seriously."

If you were peering through the window of my car, you would've seen my jaw drop. I couldn't believe what I was hearing. The rest of the conversation followed the same tone. I ended the conversation with, "I am proud of who I am and what I represent, and if my looks or being a young woman is going to affect my chances of getting a client, then maybe they aren't the right client for me."

I hung up the phone feeling infuriated, but also insanely motivated. That conversation kicked my ass into high gear, and I never looked back. Today, he is still a major contributor and mentor in my development as a speaker and author. I've found that sometimes the harshest of conversations can lead to the greatest self-improvement. That's how I saw it: a chance to be the best version of myself regardless of what others thought. I seized that defining conversation and used it as fuel, vowing to be bold and different, while remaining true to myself.

Daring to be bold, different, and unapologetically yourself will only propel you forward. Instilling these habits and a positive self-narrative will unleash the awesomeness that is you. Every time you try to fit into the mold others think you should, you are chipping away at your authenticity, which greatly affects how you show up in your life. You were put on this earth as a beautiful woman, and you should embrace every bit of your femininity. You will only elevate your potential by embracing the simple fact that *everyone* is different, and those differences are what make this world a beautiful (and interesting) place. Take courageous steps, own your unique qualities, and always show up as yourself; because you are perfect just the way you are.

I don't share this advice without having fought my way through a sea of stereotypes that have crashed against me like waves in the roughest ocean. I give you this counsel because every time I tried to fit into the mold of what was expected, I failed. I have had numerous "square peg, round hole" moments in my personal and professional lives. My success finally came when I decided to show up in a bold way, honoring my differences, and never wavering from being me.

Today, I've broken through the most male-dominated industry (automotive) to become a successful speaker, trainer, and consultant; and I was *never*, not even for one second, anyone else but myself.

In those (very) cold moments that day in my car, I swore that I would never let anyone or their perceptions of me hold me down, and neither should you.

I urge you to **BE BOLD, BE DIFFERENT, BE YOU.**

DROP THE SCARCITY MINDSET

The mean girls club exists. I have experienced it firsthand. It wasn't too long ago that a friend told me the few ladies in positions of power within the automotive industry didn't want me to succeed, and I had been "blacklisted" from a few speaking events because I wasn't part of the "in crowd." These ladies have held various positions within the industry: marketing managers, sales associates, and industry speakers. The women of the automotive industry were virtually holding my speaking career hostage because I was the new girl on the block. I, of course, thanked my friend for her honesty.

I was bewildered by this conversation. It's bad enough that women have to fight an uphill battle to attain equality, but also battling against other women is a disgrace. How are we going to win the war on equality if women don't support, guide, and refer each other?

This world is full of opportunities. Unfortunately, for women, there are fewer of these opportunities to obtain; or are there? Being a female entrepreneur has widened my eyes to the lack of opportunity we create for others and ourselves because we approach opportunities from a place of scarcity. I have found that when an opportunity presents itself, we hold it close, as if someone is going to steal it right from under our noses. Worse than that, there is a lack of support, encouragement, and referrals between women because the fear that there are not enough opportunities holds us hostage. This fear cultivates a scarcity mindset, the belief that there will never be enough—whether it's money, food, emotions, or opportunities for women to succeed.

The day I found out that I had been "blacklisted," it lit a flame inside me. I now have a burning passion to stop the scarcity mindset among women (and humans, in general) by being radically honest and having the tough conversations most are afraid to have. But more important, I will show up with an abundance mindset, helping those that cross my path.

Acting with a scarcity mindset only limits the abundance the world has to offer, not only for yourself but also for the women that surround you. As women, we often do this without knowing it; we do this because we are afraid to miss an opportunity for ourselves. We have been conditioned this way. Only 21 percent of C-suite executives are female, after all. Imagine a world, however, where we lift each other up, pass opportunities to each other, and celebrate in other women's successes. The world would be full of encouragement, new chances to succeed, and more women at the top. Abundance provides a positive ripple effect, whereas a scarcity mindset stops you dead in your tracks. To which world would you rather contribute?

If you could break one habit, stop thinking with a scarcity mindset. By thinking bigger than yourself, you will not only help others succeed, but you will also intensify your future opportunities.

Remember, actions speak louder than words. Not just for companies, but for female employees as well. Push past your fears and excuses and take the actions needed to attain your goals. Make the relationships you need to make with *both* men and women. The fact is, men are still at the top. Without their sponsorship, we will never reach the top of the incredibly steep mountain of challenges set in front of us.

I believe a leader without followers is just someone taking a walk. Similarly to the women's movement, we need men to join and follow our movement or we will be just a bunch of girls taking a walk together. Nurture the men who believe in equality and encourage them to bring their male coworkers along with them. Don't feel afraid to be in a room full of men: you'll stand out better that way. Have the confidence that you, regardless of your sex or race, deserve to be at the table and *show* them why you are. Take control of your future and take the actions needed to help the women that will walk in the path you have created. Don't wait for your company's culture to change, or for them to create a program to close the diversity gap. Be the bold trailblazer. Gather sponsorship from both men and women and start laying the stepping stones for a cultural shift. Make change happen!

FE + MALE

I believe that unless we have men joining our walk toward equality in business, equality will never happen. A man's strengths may not be those of a woman and vice versa, but together we are stronger. So, gentlemen, if you see a woman who needs mentorship, or come across the opportunity to elevate a female, do it. Be part of the movement, because without you we will be a group of women fighting an uphill battle that isn't necessary. And ladies, when you see a man reaching out his hand to help, praise him. Let the world know. By doing this, other men will feel more comfortable and confident to join the movement. Let's do this! Be the change you want to see in the world.

We need both women and men to join in the fight. Not only is elevating the professional role of women advantageous for society as a whole, but company bottom lines will flourish as a result. The men who get on board with this movement to promote females in business will show their customers and staff that they are modern, forward thinking, and trustworthy; and so is the brand they represent. It makes sense that the world's most influential consumer—the female—would view a company that advances women in a more positive light, which benefits not only a company's reputation, but the P&L report as well.

CustomHer Experience

*W*omen are the Chief Purchasing Officers, and considering that females are earning more diplomas at colleges, taking over traditional male roles in the workplace, and making more money, it is in the interest of brands in all industries to pay attention to the influence the decision maker has on the success of the brand and the world's economy. There are no signs of this trend of significant female influence abating, but only growing stronger, so the future of branding and the brand experience should remain focused on the female consumer. If you want to increase your revenue, reputation, loyalty, and future customers, then it's high time you start earning her business.

My hope is that you have been armed with the knowledge you need to tailor your brand experience to the decision maker, the woman. Now you can move into action and begin the changes that will improve the experience the most influential consumer group receives—and as a result, change your company's bottom line.

In the digital age, we get so wrapped up in the latest technology that unfortunately, we forget that we are in the people business. People want (now more than ever) human interaction. With 65 percent of Americans preferring to visit a physical store—and of those, 50 percent of millennials prefer brick-and-mortar stores as their primary means of shopping—the connection you create with your customers should not be forgotten.[1] Also, according to Gender Marketing Strategies, women are 25 to 30 percent more likely than men to make referrals.[2] Knowing that women crave connection more than men, it is essential that you connect with the Chief Purchasing Officer, the decision maker. Making an effort to get out of your comfort zone and realizing the impact she has on the success of your business will not only create excitement within your organization but will also show your female consumers that they matter. When they feel like they matter, they will want to do business with you.

Any way you slice the cake, women are becoming increasingly more comfortable and confident with being uncomfortable by taking risks and putting themselves in front of others. My prediction is that the number of women who will have enough confidence to walk through their fears and take what they want will skyrocket. This means women will make more money, rise to greater positions of power within business, and as a result, gain even more purchasing power. As a consumer, she is going to become very unapologetic about the money she spends on herself or those she loves.

We all play a part in the evolution of her purchasing power. We must support this evolution, starting in the home. Children (young boys and girls) need to see their fathers support the growth of their mothers. By doing this, we will shape our future generation to expect equality. At work, I challenge the men in executive positions to show the men in your company what it looks like to support women in the workplace.

Actions speak louder than words. Whether you like it or not, women will swim upstream and will battle it out, so you might as well put out your hand and help them. Remember, women want to do business with organizations that they could see themselves working for—businesses that care. Don't you want a slice of that cake?

Then make earning her business a priority and be willing to put in the hard work.

ACKNOWLEDGMENTS

$\mathcal{B}$ecoming an author was a pipe dream until I attended my first National Speakers Association meeting. I was in a session that outlined the impact that having content published has on a speaker's career, and I relived my internal debate on whether or not I was capable of taking the knowledge I possessed and wrapping it up with a bow in the form of a book. Little did I know that the man sitting beside me during the session would make that pipe dream a reality! Justin, thank you for seeing potential in me and helping me craft my book idea.

To my team at Greenleaf Book Group, you have been an extraordinary partner on my journey. Erin and Jessica, without your guidance, support, and gentle nudging, I would not be typing these acknowledgments right now.

Much gratitude is also owed to the mentors in my life. There are many, but I must mention a few personally. John DiJulius: without you, I might not be where I am today. Thank you for seeing fire in me and taking the time to nurture the spark that has grown. Neen James: you are simply *fabulous* and have had my back from the get-go. Thank you, Ted Ings: you were the first to join my crazy attempt at changing the automotive industry and supported me in bringing the female consumer to the forefront of conversations throughout the industry.

To my grandpa, the greatest storyteller I know: you have inspired me and lifted my spirits every step of the way. And Gram, your listening ear has helped me walk unencumbered across the finish line.

To my mom, stepdad, dad, granny, sister, brother-in-law, brother, sister-in-law, and Jolly: thank you for believing in me even when I had the craziest ideas flying around at lightning speed.

To the three ladies in my life: each a pillar of strength and support. Sandy, your friendship has kept me on track, but more important, your determination in life has inspired me to fight every obstacle put in my path. Susain, your wisdom and open mind have guided me through the roughest of waters. Shantelle, your unconditional love for me (and wine) has been felt from the day we met. We are stronger in numbers, and you three women are my stability when I don't have it.

Thayne, thank you for being you and loving me. You have been the pillar of strength I didn't know I needed, with your unlimited support and countless hours of listening to me hem and haw over the book title and cover, all while sharing my excitement over my dream becoming a reality!

And last but not least. I have an immense amount of gratitude for my children, who supported me while I wrote on vacations, weekends, and evenings. I am one lucky mommy.

NOTES

PREFACE

1. "Women Business Owner Statistics," National Association of Women Business Owners. https://www.nawbo.org/resources/women-business-owner-statistics.

INTRODUCTION

1. Jennifer Alsever, "4 Ways to Successfully Market Tech to Women," *Inc.*, April 2014. https://www.inc.com/magazine/201404/jennifer-alsever/tech-companies-market-to-female-audience.html.

2. "Women Influence 83% of all Consumer Spending in U.S.," Inclusionary Leadership Group, February 10, 2017. http://www.genderleadershipgroup.com/the-inclusionary-leadership-blog/210.

3. Neil Parker, "Gender Marketing Strategies in the Referral Space," Buyapowa, April 5, 2016. https://rewardstream.com/blog/gender-marketing-strategies-referral-space/.

4. LeanIn.org and McKinsey & Company, "Women in the Workplace," 2021, https://wiw-report.s3.amazonaws.com/Women_in_the_Workplace_2021.pdf.

5. Frost and Sullivan, "Global Female Income to Reach $24 Trillion in 2020, says Frost & Sullivan," Cision PR Newswire, March 6, 2020, https://www.prnewswire.com/in/news-releases/global-female-income-to-reach-24-trillion-in-2020-says-frost-amp-sullivan-846488109.html.

6. Gabe Rosenberg, "Study: 91 Percent of Women Feel Misunderstood by Advertisers," *The Content Strategist* (blog), July 1, 2014. https://contently.com/2014/07/01/study-91-percent-of-women-feel-misunderstood-by-advertisers/.

7. "Statistics on the Purchasing Power of Women," Girl Power Marketing. https://girlpowermarketing.com/statistics-purchasing-power-women/.

CHAPTER 1

1. Kara Cooney, "Women Achieved Enormous Power in Ancient Egypt. What They Did with It Is a Warning for Today," *Time*, October 18, 2018. https://time.com/5425216/ancient-egypt-women-in-power-today/.

2. Kerry Close, "The 10 Richest Women of All Time," *Money*, February 1, 2016. https://money.com/10-richest-women-all-time/.

3. Bob Bianchi, "Cleopatra the Great: Last Power of the Ptolemaic Dynasty," American Research Center in Egypt. https://www.arce.org/resource/cleopatra-great-last-power-ptolemaic-dynasty.

4. Kerry Close, "The 10 Richest Women of All Time."

5. M. P. Connelly, "Women in the Labour Force," The Canadian Encyclopedia, March 4, 2015. https://www.thecanadianencyclopedia.ca/en/article/women-in-the-labour-force.

6. "American Women in World War II: On the Home Front and Beyond," The National WWII Museum. https://www.nationalww2museum.org/students-teachers/student-resources/research-starters/women-wwii.

7. "Women in the Workplace 2019," Lean In. https://leanin.org/women-in-the-workplace-2019.

8. Katarzyna Sekścińska, Agata Trzcińska, and Dominika A. Maison, "The Influence of Different Social Roles Activation on Women's Financial and Consumer Choices," *Frontiers in Psychology*, March 17, 2016. https://www.frontiersin.org/articles/10.3389/fpsyg.2016.00365/full.

9. "Behind the Numbers: The State of Women-Owned Businesses in 2018," The Women's Business Enterprise National Council (WBENC). https://www.wbenc.org/blog-posts/2018/10/10/behind-the-numbers-the-state-of-women-owned-businesses-in-2018.

10. Michael J. Silverstein and Kate Sayre, "The Female Economy," *Harvard Business Review*, September 2009. https://hbr.org/2009/09/the-female-economy.

11. "Today's Primary Shopper," Private Label Manufacturers Association, 2013. https://plma.com/2013PLMA_GfK_Study.pdf.

12. Kayla Lounsbery, "Editorial: Healthcare's Primary Decision-Maker Is Female," NRC Health, March 30, 2018. https://nrchealth.com/editorial-healthcares-primary-decision-maker-female.

13. Marti Barletta, *Marketing to Women* (New York: Kaplan, 2007).

14. Sander Bosman, "Women Account for 46% of All Game Enthusiasts: Watching Game Video Content and Esports Has Changed How Women and Men Alike Engage with Games," NewZoo, May 10, 2019. https://newzoo.com/insights/articles/women-account-for-46-of-all-game-enthusiasts-watching-game-video-content-and-esports-has-changed-how-women-and-men-alike-engage-with-games/.

15. "Statistics on the Purchasing Power of Women," Girl Power Marketing. https://girlpowermarketing.com/statistics-purchasing-power-women/.

16. Cecelia Townes, "Women Impact the Bottom Line of the Sports World in Major Ways," *Forbes*, October 28, 2019. https://www.forbes.com/sites/ceceliatownes/2019/10/28/women-impact-the-bottom-line-of-the-sports-world-in-major-ways/#7a50e8814109.

17. Michael J. Silverstein and Kate Sayre, "The Female Economy."

18. Jennifer Libin, "What Women Car Shoppers Want," Wards Auto, May 05, 2016. https://www.wardsauto.com/dealer/what-women-car-shoppers-want.

19. Jenni Newman, "It's True! Women Really Do Shop More . . . for Cars," *Forbes*, May 30, 2019. https://www.forbes.com/sites/jennifernewman/2019/05/30/its-true-women-really-do-shop-more-for-cars/#1192ba493a0c.

20. Michael J. Silverstein and Kate Sayre, "The Female Economy."

21. Joseph F. Coughlin, "How Marketers Badly Misunderstand Older Female Consumers," *Forbes*, November 7, 2017. https://www.forbes.com/sites/nextavenue/2017/11/07/how-marketers-badly-misunderstand-older-female-consumers/#43d01290a2fa.

22. Amy Buckner Chowdhry, "Tech's Failure to Reach Women Costs the Industry Billions," *Entrepreneur*, January 29, 2018. https://www.entrepreneur.com/article/308057.

23. Meghan Casserly, "Dell's Revamped 'Della' Site for Women," *Forbes*, May 22, 2009. https://www.forbes.com/2009/05/22/dell-tech-marketing-forbes-woman-time-della.html#795032876256.

24. "BIC for Her Fashion Retractable Ball Pen, Medium Point, 1.0mm, Assorted-Fashion Ink, 2 Count (FHAP21-ASST)." https://www.amazon.com/BIC-Fashion-Retractable-Assorted-Fashion-FHAP21-ASST/dp/B005YGLA5Y.

25. "What We Can Learn from Marketing-To-Women Fails and Successes," Venus, January 13, 2016. https://www.venuscomms.com/what-we-can-learn-from-marketing-to-women-fails-and-successes/.

26. Micha Lally, "20 of the Biggest Marketing Fails of All Time (and Why They Sucked)," Bluleadz, August 6, 2018. https://www.bluleadz.com/blog/10-of-the-biggest-marketing-fails-of-2017.

27. Mark Sweney, "Brewdog's Pink 'Beer for Girls' Criticised as Marketing Stunt," *The Guardian*, March 6, 2018. https://www.theguardian.com/business/2018/mar/06/brewdog-pink-beer-for-girls-punk-ipa.

28. Kate Taylor, "A Cult Craft Brewer Says Its 'Beer for Girls' Is Satire— But Women Are Slamming the Company for the 'Lazy Stunt,'" *Business Insider*, March 6, 2018. https://www.businessinsider.com/brewdogs-beer-for-girls-inspires-backlash-2018-3.

CHAPTER 2

1. Sahab Uddin, "Brain Chemistry and Sex Differences: Are Male and Female Brains Really Varied?" *Journal of Neuroscience and Neuropharmacology*, August 21, 2017. https://www.omicsonline.org/open-access/brain-chemistry-and-sex-differences-are-male-and-female-brains-really-varied-100441.html.

2. Catherine Griffin, "Why Women Talk More Than Men: Language Protein Uncovered," *Science World Report*, February 20, 2013. https://www.scienceworldreport.com/articles/5073/20130220/why-women-talk-more-men-language-protein.htm.

3. Ekaterina Walter, "The top 30 statistics you need to know when marketing to women," TNW, January 24, 2012. https://thenextweb.com/socialmedia/2012/01/24/the-top-30-stats-you-need-to-know-when-marketing-to-women/.

4. "State of the Media—The Social Media Report 2012," Nielsen Global, December 4, 2012. http://www.nielsen.com/us/en/reports/2012/state-of-the-media-the-social-media-report-2012.html.

5. Rick Nauert, "Effects of 'Love Hormone' Differ Between Genders," Psych Central, August 1, 2013. https://psychcentral.com/news/2013/08/01/effects-of-love-hormone-differ-between-genders/57861.html.

6. "Male-Female Brain Differences," https://www.doctorhugo.org/brain4.html.

CHAPTER 3

1. William J. Mcewen and John H. Fleming, "Customer Satisfaction Doesn't Count," Gallup, March 13, 2003. https://news.gallup.com/businessjournal/1012/customer-satisfaction-doesnt-count.aspx.

2. Trevor Haynes, "Dopamine, Smartphones & You: A Battle for Your Time," Harvard University: Science in the News, May 1, 2018. http://sitn.hms.harvard.edu/flash/2018/dopamine-smartphones-battle-time/.

3. Rita Watson, "Oxytocin: The Love and Trust Hormone Can Be Deceptive," *Psychology Today*, October 14, 2013. https://www.psychologytoday.com/us/blog/love-and-gratitude/201310/oxytocin-the-love-and-trust-hormone-can-be-deceptive.

4. Melissa Dahl, "Yes, Shopping Can Be Addictive," *Elle*, January 6, 2017. https://www.elle.com/fashion/shopping/a41845/shopping-dopamine/.

5. Nancy R. Buchan, Rachel T.A. Croson, and Sara J. Solnick, "Trust and Gender: An Examination of Behavior and Beliefs in the Investment Game," *Journal of Economic Behavior & Organization*, December 2008. https://www.researchgate.net/publication/222329553_Trust_and_Gender_An_Examination_of_Behavior_and_Beliefs_in_the_Investment_Game.

6. Rita Watson, "Oxytocin."

7. "State of the American Workplace," Gallup, 2017. https://qualityincentivecompany.com/wp-content/uploads/2017/02/SOAW-2017.pdf.

8. Daniel Newman, "Customer Experience Is the Future Of Marketing," Forbes, October 13, 2015. https://www.forbes.com/sites/danielnewman/2015/10/13/customer-experience-is-the-future-of-marketing/#11e1975f193d.

9. Taylor Landis, "Customer Retention Marketing vs. Customer Acquisition Marketing," Outbound Engine, February 28, 2019. https://www.outboundengine.com/blog/customer-retention-marketing-vs-customer-acquisition-marketing/.

10. Hélène Tzieropoulos, Rolando Grave de Peralta, Peter Bossaerts, and Sara L. Gonzalez Andino, "The Impact of Disappointment in Decision Making: Inter-Individual Differences and Electrical Neuroimaging," *Frontiers in Human Neuroscience*, 2010. https://www.ncbi.nlm.nih.gov/pmc/articles/PMC3020567/.

11. "Male Brain vs. Female Brain: 20 Differences, Backed by Science," Learning Mind. https://www.learning-mind.com/male-brain-vs-female-brain-20-differences/.

12. University of California, Irvine, "Intelligence in Men and Women Is a Gray and White Matter," ScienceDaily. https://www.sciencedaily.com/releases/2005/01/050121100142.htm.

13. Jill Anonson, "3 Steps for Effective Customer Engagement," Ita Group. https://www.itagroup.com/insights/3-steps-for-effective-customer-engagement.

CHAPTER 4

1. Gabe Rosenberg, "Study: 91 Percent of Women Feel Misunderstood by Advertisers," The Content Strategist, July 1, 2014. https://contently.com/2014/07/01/study-91-percent-of-women-feel-misunderstood-by-advertisers/.

2. James Allen, Frederick F. Reichheld, Barney Hamilton, and Rob Markey, "Closing the Delivery Gap: How to Achieve True Customer-Led Growth," Bain & Company, October 5, 2005. https://www.bain.com/insights/closing-the-delivery-gap-newsletter/.

CHAPTER 5

1. Dom Nicastro, "5 Customer Experience Trends to Watch," CMSWire, April 11, 2018. https://www.cmswire.com/customer-experience/5-customer-experience-trends-to-watch/.

CHAPTER 6

1. Maria Andersson, Sara Palmblad, and Tajana Prevedan, "Atmospheric Effects on Hedonic and Utilitarian Customers," Linnæus University, Spring 2012. http://www.diva-portal.org/smash/get/diva2:531689/FULLTEXT02.

2. Terry L. Childers, Christopher L. Carr, Joann Peck, and Stephen Carson, "Hedonic and Utilitarian Motivations for Online Retail Shopping Behavior," *Journal of Retailing*, Winter 2001. https://www.sciencedirect.com/science/article/abs/pii/S0022435901000562.

3. Carlota Lorenzo-Romero, Miguel-Ángel Gómez-Borja, and Alejandro Mollá-Descals, "Effects of Utilitarian and Hedonic Atmospheric Dimensions on Consumer Responses in an Online Shopping Environment," *African Journal*

of Business Management, September 23, 2011. https://pdfs.semanticscholar. org/465b/4f7659d25a4b9b56ab885cfb99b77da308c2.pdf.

4. "Women vs. Men—Gender Differences in Purchase Decision Making," Zoovu, October 29, 2015. https://zoovu.com/blog/ women-vs-men-gender-differences-in-purchase-decision-making/.

5. John Gray, *Men Are from Mars, Women Are from Venus* (New York: HarperCollins, 2012).

6. Magdalena Śmieja, Jarosław Orzechowski, and Maciej S. Stolarski, "TIE: An Ability Test of Emotional Intelligence," *PLoS One*, 2014. https://www.ncbi.nlm. nih.gov/pmc/articles/PMC4114749/.

7. Magdalena Śmieja et al., "TIE."

CHAPTER 7

1. Vivian Hunt, Dennis Layton, and Sara Prince, "Why Diversity Matters," McKinsey & Company, January 2015. https://www.mckinsey.com/ business-functions/organization/our-insights/why-diversity-matters.

2. Alex Hisaka, "Trends of Women in Sales Infographic," LinkedIn, June 24, 2014. https://business.linkedin.com/sales-solutions/blog/t/ trends-of-women-in-sales-infographic.

3. George Guilder, "Women in the Work Force," *The Atlantic*, September 1986. https://www.theatlantic.com/magazine/archive/1986/09/ women-in-the-work-force/304924/.

4. Dina Gerdeman, "Why Employers Favor Men," Harvard Business School: Working Knowledge, September 11, 2017. https://hbswk.hbs.edu/item/ why-employers-favor-men.

5. LeanIn.org and McKinsey & Company, "Women in the Workplace," 2021, https://wiw-report.s3.amazonaws.com/Women_in_the_Workplace_ 2021.pdf.

6. Vivian Huntet et al., "Why Diversity Matters."

7. Sharon Silke Carty, "The 'Extra Oomph' That Changed GM," *Automotive News*, October 22, 2017. https://www.autonews.com/article/20171022/ OEM02/171029979/the-extra-oomph-that-changed-gm.

8. Loren Mooney, "Mary Barra: 'I'm Not in a Startup, but a Start-Over,'" Stanford Business, May 27, 2014. https://www.gsb.stanford.edu/insights/ mary-barra-im-not-startup-start-over.

9. Jess Huang, Alexis Krivkovich, Irina Starikova, Lareina Yee, and Delia Zanoschi, "Women in the Workplace 2019," McKinsey & Company, October 2019. https://www.mckinsey.com/featured-insights/gender-equality/women-in-the-workplace-2019.

CHAPTER 8

1. "Gender Equality in the Workplace," Gender Equality Funds. https://genderequalityfunds.org/gender-equality-workplace.

2. "Women in the Workplace 2019," Lean In. https://leanin.org/women-in-the-workplace-2019.

3. Jess Huang, Alexis Krivkovich, Irina Starikova, Lareina Yee, and Delia Zanoschi, "Women in the Workplace 2019," McKinsey & Company, October 2019. https://www.mckinsey.com/featured-insights/gender-equality/women-in-the-workplace-2019.

4. Minda Zetlin, "54 Percent of Women Report Workplace Harassment. How Is Your Company Responding?," *Inc.*, March 2018. https://www.inc.com/magazine/201804/minda-zetlin/sexual-harassment-workplace-policy-metoo.html.

5. Ksenia Keplinger, Stefanie K. Johnson, Jessica F. Kirk, and Liza Y. Barnes, "Women at Work: Changes in Sexual Harassment Between September 2016 and September 2018," *PLoS One*, July 17, 2019. https://www.ncbi.nlm.nih.gov/pmc/articles/PMC6636712/.

6. Mark DeWolf, "12 Stats About Working Women," U.S. Department of Labor (blog), March 1, 2017. https://blog.dol.gov/2017/03/01/12-stats-about-working-women.

7. "International Women's Day Sailing," Celebrity Cruises. https://www.celebritycruises.com/ca/about-us/celebrity-cares/international-womens-day.

8. Tara Sophia Mohr, "Why Women Don't Apply for Jobs Unless They're 100% Qualified," *Harvard Business Review*, August 25, 2014. https://hbr.org/2014/08/why-women-dont-apply-for-jobs-unless-theyre-100-qualified.

9. Bill Merrick, "3 steps to strategic storytelling," CUInsight. https://www.cuinsight.com/3-steps-strategic-storytelling.html.

CHAPTER 9

1. Og Madino, *The Greatest Salesman in the World* (New York: Bantam, 1983).

CHAPTER 10

1. Stacia Damron, "Workplace Trust—58% of People Trust Strangers More than Their Own Boss" (blog), One Model. https://www.onemodel.co/blog/workplace-trust.

2. "Mind the Workplace," Mental Health America, Inc., 2017. https://www.mhanational.org/sites/default/files/Mind%20the%20Workplace%20-%20MHA%20Workplace%20Health%20Survey%202017%20FINAL.pdf.

3. Jim Harter and Annamarie Mann, "The Right Culture: Not Just About Employee Satisfaction," Gallup, April 12, 2017. https://www.gallup.com/workplace/236366/right-culture-not-employee-satisfaction.aspx.

4. Bulent Osman, "Reversing Low Employee Engagement In Manufacturing," Forbes. https://www.forbes.com/sites/forbestechcouncil/2018/04/17/reversing-low-employee-engagement-in-manufacturing/#1419ebe528f0.

5. "How Long Does It Really Take to Break a Habit?" (blog), Blackmores. https://www.blackmores.com.au/everyday-health/how-long-does-it-really-take-to-break-a-habit.

CONCLUSION

1. "Millennials Prefer Shopping In-Store, According to New SmarterHQ Survey," SmarterHQ. https://smarterhq.com/blog/millennials-prefer-shopping-in-store-according-to-new-smarterhq-survey.

2. Neil Parker, "Gender Marketing Strategies in the Referral Space," Buyapowa, April 5, 2016. https://rewardstream.com/blog/gender-marketing-strategies-referral-space/.

ABOUT THE AUTHOR

*A*s a brand experience expert, Katie knows firsthand the challenges organizations encounter as they strive to design a sustainable and effective CX program tailored for the female consumer. Using her experiences as a Chief Inspiration Officer, building company infrastructure, and designing customer experience programs, she is now a leading voice for positive, actionable change in the organizations with which she partners. Katie has a master's degree in Adult Training and Development from Schulich School of Business and a Certified Training and Development Professional (CTDP) certification.

As a highly sought-after speaker, Katie has inspired audiences around the world to think differently about the female consumer, customer experience, and leadership. She has worked with globally recognized brands, including Honda, Celebrity Cruises, and Canada Post.

Katie and her fiancé have seven children (a Brady Bunch sorta thing), and she lives in three countries. When she is not with her kiddos, she has her toes in the sand and a fly rod in her hand. Katie really believes in living life to the fullest so she and her family can have their cake and eat it too!